Workshop on Extraction of Structured Knowledge from Scientific Publications (ESSP 2019)

Minneapolis, Minnesota, USA
6 June 2019

ISBN: 978-1-5108-8780-0

Printed from e-media with permission by:

Curran Associates, Inc.
57 Morehouse Lane
Red Hook, NY 12571

Some format issues inherent in the e-media version may also appear in this print version.

Printed by Curran Associates, Inc. (2019)

For permission requests, please contact the Association for Computational Linguistics
at the address below.

Association for Computational Linguistics
209 N. Eighth Street
Stroudsburg, Pennsylvania 18360

Phone: 1-570-476-8006
Fax: 1-570-476-0860

acl@aclweb.org

Additional copies of this publication are available from:

Curran Associates, Inc.
57 Morehouse Lane
Red Hook, NY 12571 USA
Phone: 845-758-0400
Fax: 845-758-2633
Email: curran@proceedings.com
Web: www.proceedings.com

NAACL HLT 2019

**Extraction of Structured Knowledge
from Scientific Publications
ESSP**

Proceedings of the Workshop

June 6th, 2019
Minneapolis, USA

Empirical Linguistics
and Computational Language Modeling

Introduction

Scientific knowledge is one of the greatest assets of humankind. This knowledge is recorded and disseminated in scientific publications, and the body of scientific literature is growing at an enormous rate. Automatic methods of processing and cataloguing that information are necessary for assisting scientists to navigate this vast amount of information, and for facilitating automated reasoning, discovery and decision making on that data.

Structured information can be extracted at different levels of granularity. Previous and ongoing work has focused on bibliographic information (segmentation and linking of referenced literature), keyword extraction and categorization (e.g., what are tasks, materials and processes central to a publication), and cataloguing research findings. Scientific discoveries can often be represented as pairwise relationships, e.g., protein-protein, drug-drug, and chemical-disease interactions, or as more complicated networks such as action graphs describing scientific procedures (e.g., synthesis recipes in material sciences). Information extracted with such methods can be enriched with time-stamps, and other meta-information, such as indicators of uncertainty or limitations of the discovered facts.

Structured representations, such as knowledge graphs, summarize information from a variety of sources in a convenient and machine readable format. Graph representations that link the information of a large body of publications can reveal patterns and lead to the discovery of new information that would not be apparent from the analysis of just one publication, or from extracted isolated pieces of information. This kind of aggregation can lead to new scientific insights and it can also help to detect trends or find experts for a particular scientific area.

While various workshops have focused separately on several aspects – extraction of information from scientific articles, building and using knowledge graphs, the analysis of bibliographical information, graph algorithms for text analysis – the aim of the ESSP workshop is to elicit and stimulate work that targets the extraction and aggregation of structured information, and to ultimately lead to finding novel information and scientific discoveries.

We have received 15 submissions, of which we accepted 10: 5 for oral presentation, 4 as posters and one demo. The topics covered the biomedical domain, mathematics, computer science and general science, with approaches focusing on various aspects of the extraction, learning, and knowledge processing.

To complement the accepted papers, we welcome four invited speakers from industry, state institutions and academia, to provide insights into knowledge requirements and state of the art in specific fields (medicine, social sciences) and contexts:

Michael Cafarella
> University of Michigan
> *Extraction-Intensive Systems for the Social Sciences*

Dina Demner-Fushman
> National Library of Medicine
> *Extracting structured knowledge from biomedical publications*

Hoifung Poon
> Director, Precision Health NLP @ Microsoft
> *Machine Reading for Precision Medicine*

Chris Welty
> Google Research
> *Just when I thought I was out, they pull me back in – The role of KG in AKBC*

We thank our authors, speakers and program committee members for helping us assemble an exciting program on this timely topic. We are grateful to our sponsors – BASF SE Ludwigshafen, the Leibniz Science Campus "Empirical Linguistics and Computational Language Modeling" (LiMo), the German Research Foundation (DFG grant RO5127/2-1) – for making such a diverse and speaker-rich program possible.

Vivi Nastase, Benjamin Roth, Laura Dietz, Andrew McCallum

Organizers:

Vivi Nastase, University of Heidelberg
Benjamin Roth, Ludwig Maximilian University of Munich
Laura Dietz, University of New Hampshire
Andrew McCallum, University of Massachusetts Amherst

Program Committee:

Rabah Al-Zaidy, KAUST, Saudi Arabia
Sergio Baranzini, UCSF
Ken Barker, IBM
Chaitan Baru, UCSD
Chandra Bhagavatula, Allen Institute for AI
Volha Bryl, Springer Nature
Trevor Cohen, MBChB
Anette Frank, University of Heidelberg
Ingo Frommholz, University of Bedfordshire
Daniel Garijo, ISI
Hannaneh Hajishirzi, University of Washington
Keith Hall, Google
Marcel Karnstedt Hulpus, Springer Semantic Web
Bhushan Kotnis, NEC Labs
Anne Lauscher, Mannheim University
Yi Luan, University of Washington
Sebastian Martschat, BASF
Philipp Mayr-Schlegel, GESIS
Arunav Mishra, BASF
Mathias Niepert, NEC Labs
Adam Roegiest, Kira Systems
Martin Schmitt, LMU Munich
Isabel Segura-Bedmar, University Carlos III of Madrid
Mihai Surdeanu, University of Arizona
Niket Tandon, Allen Institute for AI
Karin Verspoor, University of Melbourne
Gerhard Weikum, MPII Saarbruecken
Robert West, EPFL
Guido Zucchon, Queensland University

Invited Speakers:

Michael Cafarella, University of Michigan
Dina Denmer-Fushman, National Library of Medicine
Hoifung Poon, Director, Precision Health NLP @ Microsoft
Chris Welty, Google AI

Table of Contents

Workshop Program

Thursday, June 6, 2019

9:00–10:30   *Session 1*

9:00–9:15   *Welcome*

9:15–10:10   *INVITED TALK: Machine Reading for Precision Medicine*
Hoifung Poon

10:10–10:30   *Distantly Supervised Biomedical Knowledge Acquisition via Knowledge Graph Based Attention*
Qin Dai, Naoya Inoue, Paul Reisert, Ryo Takahashi and Kentaro Inui

10:30–11:00   *Coffee break*

11:00–12:30   *Session 2*

11:00–11:50   *INVITED TALK: Extraction-Intensive Systems for the Social Sciences*
Michael Cafarella

11:50–12:10   *Scalable, Semi-Supervised Extraction of Structured Information from Scientific Literature*
Kritika Agrawal, Aakash Mittal and Vikram Pudi

12:10–12:30   *Understanding the Polarity of Events in the Biomedical Literature: Deep Learning vs. Linguistically-informed Methods*
Enrique Noriega-Atala, Zhengzhong Liang, John Bachman, Clayton Morrison and Mihai Surdeanu

12:30–14:00   *Lunch break*

14:00–15:15   *Session 3*

14:00–14:50   *INVITED TALK: Extracting Structured Knowledge from Biomedical Publications*
Dina Demner-Fushman

14:50–14:55   *Dataset Mention Extraction and Classification*
Animesh Prasad, Chenglei Si and Min-Yen Kan

14:55–15:00   *Annotating with Pros and Cons of Technologies in Computer Science Papers*
Hono Shirai, Naoya Inoue, Jun Suzuki and Kentaro Inui

15:00–15:05   *Browsing Health: Information Extraction to Support New Interfaces for Accessing Medical Evidence*
Soham Parikh, Elizabeth Conrad, Oshin Agarwal, Iain Marshall, Byron Wallace and Ani Nenkova

15:05–15:10   *An Analysis of Deep Contextual Word Embeddings and Neural Architectures for Toponym Mention Detection in Scientific Publications*
Matthew Magnusson and Laura Dietz

15:10–15:15   *STAC: Science Toolkit Based on Chinese Idiom Knowledge Graph*
Meiling Wang, Min Xiao, Changliang Li, Yu Guo, Zhixin Zhao and Xiaonan Liu

15:15–16:00   Coffee break and Poster session

16:00–17:30   Session 4

16:00–16:50   *INVITED TALK: Just When I Thought I Was Out, They Pull Me Back In: The Role of Knowledge Representation in Automatic Knowledge Base Construction*
Chris Welty

16:50–17:10   *Playing by the Book: An Interactive Game Approach for Action Graph Extraction from Text*
Ronen Tamari, Hiroyuki Shindo, Dafna Shahaf and Yuji Matsumoto

17:10–17:30   *Textual and Visual Characteristics of Mathematical Expressions in Scholar Documents*
Vidas Daudaravicius

Distantly Supervised Biomedical Knowledge Acquisition via Knowledge Graph Based Attention

Qin Dai[1], Naoya Inoue[1,2], Paul Reisert[2], Ryo Takahashi[1] and Kentaro Inui[1,2]
[1]Tohoku University, Japan
[2]RIKEN Center for Advanced Intelligence Project, Japan
{daiqin, naoya-i, preisert, ryo.t, inui}@ecei.tohoku.ac.jp

Abstract

The increased demand for structured scientific knowledge has attracted considerable attention in extracting scientific relation from the ever growing scientific publications. Distant supervision is widely applied approach to automatically generate large amounts of labelled data for Relation Extraction (RE). However, distant supervision inevitably accompanies the wrong labelling problem, which will negatively affect the RE performance. To address this issue, (Han et al., 2018) proposes a novel framework for jointly training RE model and Knowledge Graph Completion (KGC) model to extract structured knowledge from non-scientific dataset. In this work, we firstly investigate the feasibility of this framework on scientific dataset, specifically on biomedical dataset. Secondly, to achieve better performance on the biomedical dataset, we extend the framework with other competitive KGC models. Moreover, we proposed a new end-to-end KGC model to extend the framework. Experimental results not only show the feasibility of the framework on the biomedical dataset, but also indicate the effectiveness of our extensions, because our extended model achieves significant and consistent improvements on distantly supervised RE as compared with baselines.

1 Introduction

Scientific Knowledge Graph (KG), such as Unified Medical Language System (UMLS) [1], is extremely crucial for many scientific Natural Language Processing (NLP) tasks such as Question Answering (QA), Information Retrieval (IR), Relation Extraction (RE), etc. Scientific KG provides large collections of relations between entities, typically stored as (h, r, t) triplets, where $h = head$ entity, $r = $ relation and $t = tail\ entity$, e.g., (acetaminophen, may_treat, pain). However, as with general KGs such as Freebase (Bollacker et al., 2008) and DBpedia (Lehmann et al., 2015), scientific KGs are far from complete and this would impede their usefulness in real-world applications. Scientific KGs, on the one hand, face the data sparsity problem. On the other hand, scientific publications have become the largest repository ever for scientific KGs and continue to increase at an unprecedented rate (Munroe, 2013). Therefore, it is an essential and fundamental task to turn the unstructured scientific publications into well organized KG, and it belongs to the task of RE.

In RE, one obstacle that is encountered when building a RE system is the generation of training instances. For coping with this difficulty, (Mintz et al., 2009) proposes distant supervision to automatically generate training samples via leveraging the alignment between KGs and texts. They assumes that if two entities are connected by a relation in a KG, then all sentences that contain these entity pairs will express the relation. For instance, (aspirin, may_treat, pain) is a fact triplet in UMLS. Distant supervision will automatically label all sentences, such as Example 1, Example 2 and Example 3, as positive instances for the relation may_treat. Although distant supervision could provide a large amount of training data at low cost, it always suffers from wrong labelling problem. For instance, comparing to Example 1, Example 2 and Example 3 should not be seen as the evidences to support the may_treat relationship between aspirin and pain, but will still be annotated as positive instances by the distant supervision.

(1) *The clinical manifestations are generally typical nocturnal **pain** that prevents sleep and that is alleviated with **aspirin**.*

---

[1]https://www.nlm.nih.gov/research/umls/

Proceedings of the Workshop on Extracting Structured Knowledge from Scientific Publications, pages 1–10
Minneapolis, USA, June 6, 2019. ©2019 Association for Computational Linguistics

(2) *The tumor was remarkably large in size , and* **pain** *unrelieved by* **aspirin**.

(3) *The level of* **pain** *did not change significantly with either* **aspirin** *or pentoxifylline , but the walking distance was farther with the pentoxifylline group .*

To automatically alleviate the wrong labelling problem, (Riedel et al., 2010; Hoffmann et al., 2011) apply multi-instance learning. In order to avoid the handcrafted features and errors propagated from NLP tools, (Zeng et al., 2015) proposes a Convolutional Neural Network (CNN), which incorporate mutli-instance learning with neural network model, and achieves significant improvement in distantly supervised RE. Despite the impressive achievement in RE, this model still has the limitation that it only selects the most informative sentence and ignores the rest, thereby loses the rich information stored in those neglected sentences, For instance, among Example 1, Example 2 and Example 3, Example 1 is undoubtedly the most informative one for detecting relation *may_treat*, but it unnecessarily means other sentences such as Example 3 could not contribute to the relation detection. In Example 3, entity *aspirin* and entity *pentoxifylline* have alternative relation, and the latter is a drug to treat muscle pain, therefore the former is also likely to be a pain-killing drug. To address this issue, recently, attention mechanism is applied to extract features from all collected sentences. (Lin et al., 2016) proposes a relation vector based attention mechanism for distantly supervised RE. (Han et al., 2018) proposes a novel joint model that leverages the KG-based attention mechanism and achieves better performance than (Lin et al., 2016) on distantly supervised RE from New York Times (NYT) corpus.

The success that the joint model (Han et al., 2018) has attained in the newswire domain (or non-scientific domain) inspires us to choose the strong model as our base model and assess its feasibility on biomedical domain. Specifically, the first question of this research is how the joint model behaves when the system is trained on biomedical KG (e.g., UMLS) and biomeical corpus (e.g., Medline corpus). (Han et al., 2018) indicates that the performance of the base model could be affected the representation ability of KGC model. The representation ability of a KGC model also varies with dataset (Wang et al., 2017).

Therefore, given a new dataset (e.g., a biomedical dataset), it is necessary to extend the base model with other competitive KGC models, and choose the best fit for the given dataset. However, the base model only implements two KGC models, which are based on TransE (Bordes et al., 2013) and TransD (Ji et al., 2015) respectively. Thus, the second question of this work is how other competitive KGC models such as ComplEx (Trouillon et al., 2016) and SimplE (Kazemi and Poole, 2018) influence the performance of the base model on biomedical dataset. At last but not least, in biomedical KG, a relation is scientifically restricted by entity type (ET). For instance, in the relation (h, *may_treat*, t), the ET of t should be `Disease or Syndrome`. Therefore, ET information is an important feature for biomedical RE and KGC. For leveraging the ET information, which the base model lacks, in this work, we propose an end-to-end KGC model to enhance the base model. The proposed KGC model is capable of identifying ET via the word embedding of target entity and incorporating the predicted ET into a state-of-to-art KGC model to evaluate the plausibility of potential fact triplets.

We conduct evaluation on biomedical datasets in which KG is collected from UMLS and textual data is extracted from Medline corpus. The experimental results not only show the feasibility of the base model on the biomedical domain, but also prove the effectiveness of our proposed extensions for the base model.

2 Related Work

RE is a fundamental task in the NLP community. In recent years, Neural Network (NN)-based models have been the dominant approaches for non-scientific RE, which include Convolutional Neural Network (CNN)-based frameworks (Zeng et al., 2014; Xu et al., 2015; Santos et al., 2015) Recurrent Neural Network (RNN)-based frameworks (Zhang and Wang, 2015; Miwa and Bansal, 2016; Zhou et al., 2016). NN-based approaches are also used in scientific RE. For instance, (Gu et al., 2017) utilizes a CNN-based model for identifying *chemical-disease* relations from Medline corpus. (Hahn-Powell et al., 2016) proposes an LSTM-based model for identifying *causal precedence* relationship between two event mentions in biomedical papers. (Ammar et al., 2017) applies (Miwa and Bansal, 2016)'s model for scientific

RE.

Although remarkably good performances are achieved by the models mentioned above, they still train and extract relations on sentence-level and thus need a large amount of annotation data, which is expensive and time-consuming. To address this issue, distant supervision is proposed by (Mintz et al., 2009). To alleviate the noisy data from the distant supervision, many studies model distant supervision for RE as a Multiple Instance Learning (MIL) problem (Riedel et al., 2010; Hoffmann et al., 2011; Zeng et al., 2015), in which all sentences containing a target entity pair (e.g.,*aspirin* and *pain*) are seen as a bag to be classified. To make full use of all the sentences in the bag, rather than just the most informative one, (Lin et al., 2016) proposes a relation vector based attention mechanism to extract feature from the entire bag and outperforms the prior approaches. (Han et al., 2018) proposes a joint model that adopts a KG-based attention mechanism and achieves better performance than (Lin et al., 2016) on distantly supervised RE from NYT corpus.

In this work, we are primarily interested in applying distant supervision techniques to extract biomedical fact triplets from scientific publications. To validate and enhance the efficacy of the previous techniques in biomedical domain, we choose the strong joint model proposed by (Han et al., 2018) as the base model and make some necessary extension for our scientific RE task. Since from the two main groups of KGC models (Wang et al., 2017): translational distance models and semantic matching models, the base model only implements the translational distance models, TransE (Bordes et al., 2013) and TransD (Ji et al., 2015), we thus extend the base model with the semantic matching models, ComplEx (Trouillon et al., 2016) and SimplE (Kazemi and Poole, 2018), for selecting the best fit for our task. In addition, the base model has not incorporated the ET information, which we assume is crucial for scientific RE. Therefore, we propose an end-to-end KGC model to enhance the base model. Different from the work (Xie et al., 2016), which utilizes an ET look-up dictionary to obtain ET, the end-to-end KGC is capable of identifying ET via the word embedding of a target entity and thus is free of the attachment to an incomplete ET look-up dictionary.

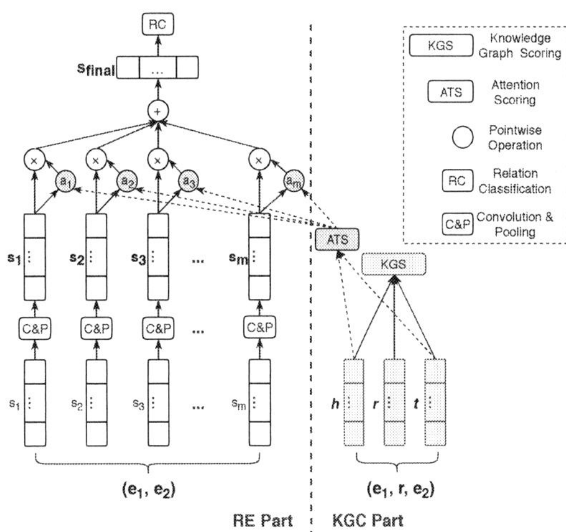

Figure 1: Overview of the base model.

3 Base Model

The architecture of the base model is illustrated in Figure 1. In this section, we will introduce the base model proposed by (Han et al., 2018) in two main parts: KGC part, RE part.

3.1 KGC Part

Suppose we have a KG containing a set of fact triplets $\mathcal{O} = \{(e_1, r, e_2)\}$, where each fact triplet consists of two entities $e_1, e_2 \in \mathcal{E}$ and their relation $r \in \mathcal{R}$. Here $\mathcal{E}$ and $\mathcal{R}$ stand for the set of entities and relations respectively. KGC model then encodes $e_1, e_2 \in \mathcal{E}$ and their relation $r \in \mathcal{R}$ into low-dimensional vectors $\mathbf{h}$, $\mathbf{t} \in R^d$ and $\mathbf{r} \in R^d$ respectively, where d is the dimensionality of the embedding space. As mentioned above, the base model adopts two representative translational distance models Prob-TransE and Prob-TransD, which are based on TransE (Bordes et al., 2013) and TransD (Ji et al., 2015) repectively, to score a fact triplet. Specifically, given an entity pair (e_1, e_2), Prob-TransE defines its latent relation embedding $\mathbf{r}_{ht}$ via the Equation 1.

$$\mathbf{r}_{ht} = \mathbf{t} - \mathbf{h} \qquad (1)$$

Prob-TransD is an extension of Prob-TransE and introduces additional mapping vectors $\mathbf{h}_p$, $\mathbf{t}_p \in R^d$ and $\mathbf{r}_p \in R^d$ for e_1, e_2 and r respectively. Prob-TransD encodes the latent relation embedding via the Equation 2, where $\mathbf{M}_{rh}$ and $\mathbf{M}_{rt}$ are projection matrices for mapping entity embeddings into relation spaces.

$$\mathbf{r}_{ht} = \mathbf{t}_r - \mathbf{h}_r, \qquad (2)$$

$$\mathbf{h}_r = \mathbf{M}_{rh}\mathbf{h},$$
$$\mathbf{t}_r = \mathbf{M}_{rt}\mathbf{t},$$
$$\mathbf{M}_{rh} = \mathbf{r}_p\mathbf{h}_p^\top + \mathbf{I}^{d\times d},$$
$$\mathbf{M}_{rt} = \mathbf{r}_p\mathbf{t}_p^\top + \mathbf{I}^{d\times d}$$

The conditional probability can be formalized over all fact triplets $\mathcal{O}$ via the Equations 3 and 4, where $f_r(e_1, e_2)$ is the KG scoring function, which is used to evaluate the plausibility of a given fact triplet. For instance, the score for (*aspirin, may_treat, pain*) would be higher than the one for (*aspirin, has_ingredient, pain*), because the former is more plausible than the latter. $\theta_\mathcal{E}$ and $\theta_\mathcal{R}$ are parameters for entities and relations respectively, b is a bias constant.

$$P(r|(e_1, e_2), \theta_\mathcal{E}, \theta_\mathcal{R}) = \frac{\exp(f_r(e_1, e_2))}{\sum_{r'\in\mathcal{R}} \exp(f_{r'}(e_1, e_2))} \tag{3}$$

$$f_r(e_1, e_2) = b - \|\mathbf{r}_{ht} - \mathbf{r}\| \tag{4}$$

3.2 RE Part

Sentence Representation Learning. Given a sentence s with n words $s = \{w_1, ..., w_n\}$ including a target entity pair (e_1, e_2), CNN is used to generate a distributed representation $\mathbf{s}$ for the sentence. Specifically, vector representation $\mathbf{v}_t$ for each word w_t is calculated via Equation 5, where $\mathbf{W}_{emb}^w$ is a word embedding projection matrix (Mikolov et al., 2013), $\mathbf{W}_{emb}^{wp}$ is a word position embedding projection matrix, $\mathbf{x}_t^w$ is a one-hot word representation and $\mathbf{x}_t^{wp}$ is a one-hot word position representation. The word position describes the relative distance between the current word and the target entity pair (Zeng et al., 2014). For instance, in the sentence "*Patients recorded pain and aspirin$_{e_1}$ consumption in a daily diary*"^{e_2}, the relative distance of the word "*and*" is [1, -1].

$$\mathbf{v}_t = [\mathbf{v}_t^w; \mathbf{v}_t^{wp1}; \mathbf{v}_t^{wp2}], \tag{5}$$

$$\mathbf{v}_t^w = \mathbf{W}_{emb}^w \mathbf{x}_t^w,$$
$$\mathbf{v}_t^{wp1} = \mathbf{W}_{emb}^{wp}\mathbf{x}_t^{wp1},$$
$$\mathbf{v}_t^{wp2} = \mathbf{W}_{emb}^{wp}\mathbf{x}_t^{wp2}$$

The distributed representation $\mathbf{s}$ is formulated via the Equation 6, where, $[\mathbf{s}]_i$ and $[\mathbf{h}_t]_i$ are the i-th value of $\mathbf{s}$ and $\mathbf{h}_t$, M is the dimensionality of $\mathbf{s}$, $\mathbf{W}$ is the convolution kernal, $\mathbf{b}$ is a bias vector, and k is the convolutional window size.

$$[\mathbf{s}]_i = \max_t\{[\mathbf{h}_t]_i\}, \; \forall i = 1, ..., M \tag{6}$$

$$\mathbf{h}_t = \tanh(\mathbf{W}\mathbf{z}_t + \mathbf{b}),$$
$$\mathbf{z}_t = [\mathbf{v}_{t-(k-1)/2}; ...; \mathbf{v}_{t+(k-1)/2}]$$

KG-based Attention. Suppose for each fact triplet (e_1, r, e_2), there might be multiple sentences $S_r = \{s_1, ..., s_m\}$ in which each sentence contains the entity pair (e_1, e_2) and is assumed to imply the relation r, m is the size of S_r. As discussed before, the distant supervision inevitably collect noisy sentences, the base model adopts a KG-based attention mechanism to discriminate the informative sentences from the noisy ones. Specifically, the base model use the latent relation embedding $\mathbf{r}_{ht}$ from Equation 1 (or Equation 2) as the attention over S_r to generate its final representation $\mathbf{s}_{final}$. $\mathbf{s}_{final}$ is calculated via Equation 7, where $\mathbf{W}_s$ is the weight matrix, $\mathbf{b}_s$ is the bias vector, a_i is the weight for $\mathbf{s}_i$, which is the distributed representation for the i-th sentence in S_r.

$$\mathbf{s}_{final} = \sum_{i=1}^m a_i\mathbf{s}_i, \tag{7}$$

$$a_i = \frac{\exp(\langle \mathbf{r}_{ht}, \mathbf{x}_i \rangle)}{\sum_{k=1}^m \exp(\langle \mathbf{r}_{ht}, \mathbf{x}_k \rangle)},$$
$$\mathbf{x}_i = \tanh(\mathbf{W}_s\mathbf{s}_i + \mathbf{b}_s)$$

Finally, the conditional probability $P(r|S_r, \theta)$ is formulated via Equation 8 and Equation 9, where, θ is the parameters for RE, which includes $\{\mathbf{W}_{emb}^w, \mathbf{W}_{emb}^{wp}, \mathbf{W}, \mathbf{b}, \mathbf{W}_s, \mathbf{b}_s, \mathbf{M}, \mathbf{d}\}$, $\mathbf{M}$ is the representation matrix of relations, $\mathbf{d}$ is a bias vector, $\mathbf{o}$ is the output vector containing the prediction probabilities of all target relations for the input sentences set S_r, and n_r is the total number of relations.

$$P(r|S_r, \theta) = \frac{\exp(\mathbf{o}_r)}{\sum_{c=1}^{n_r} \exp(\mathbf{o}_c)} \tag{8}$$

$$\mathbf{o} = \mathbf{M}\mathbf{s}_{final} + \mathbf{d} \tag{9}$$

4 Extensions

The base model opens the possibility to jointly train RE models with KGC models for distantly supervised RE. The empirical results of the base model on NYT corpus indicate that the performance of distantly supervised RE varies with KGC models (Han et al., 2018). In addition, the performance of KGC models depends on a given dataset (Wang et al., 2017). Therefore, we assume that it is necessary to attempt multiple competitive KGC models for the joint framework so as to find the optimal combination for our biomedical dataset. However, the base model only implements translational distance models: TransE and TransD, but not the semantic matching models, and this, we assume, might hinder its performance in the new dataset. To address this, we select two representative semantic matching models: ComplEx (Trouillon et al., 2016) and SimplE (Kazemi and Poole, 2018) as the alternative KGC part.

As discussed in Section 1, in scientific KGs, a fact triplet is severely restricted by ET information (e.g., ET of e_2 should be `Disease or Syndrome` in the fact triplet (e_1, may_treat, e_2)). Therefore, for leveraging ET information, which the base model lacks, we also propose an end-to-end KGC model to extend the base model. Since the proposed KGC model is build on SimplE and is capable of Named Entity Recognition (NER), we call it SimplE_NER.

4.1 ComplEx based Attention

Given a fact triplet (e_1, r, e_2), ComplEx then encodes entities e_1, e_2 and relation r into a complex-valued vector $\mathbf{e}_1 \in C^d$, $\mathbf{e}_2 \in C^d$ and $\mathbf{r} \in C^d$ respectively, where d is the dimensionality of the embedding space. Since entities and relations are represented as complex-valued vector, each $\mathbf{x} \in C^d$ consists of a real vector component $Re(\mathbf{x})$ and imaginary vector component $Im(\mathbf{x})$, namely $\mathbf{x} = Re(\mathbf{x}) + iIm(\mathbf{x})$. The KG scoring function of ComplEx for a fact triplet (e_1, r, e_2) is calculated via Equation 10, where $\bar{\mathbf{e}}_2$ is the conjugate of $\mathbf{e}_2$; $Re(\cdot)$ (or $Im(\cdot)$) means taking the real (or imaginary) part of a complex value. $\langle u, v, w \rangle$ is defined via Equation 11, where $[\cdot]_n$ is the n-th entry of a vector.

$$f_r(e_1, e_2) = Re(\langle \mathbf{e}_1, \mathbf{r}, \bar{\mathbf{e}}_2 \rangle) = \\ \langle Re(\mathbf{r}), Re(\mathbf{e}_1), Re(\mathbf{e}_2) \rangle \\ + \langle Re(\mathbf{r}), Im(\mathbf{e}_1), Im(\mathbf{e}_2) \rangle \\ + \langle Im(\mathbf{r}), Re(\mathbf{e}_1), Im(\mathbf{e}_2) \rangle \\ - \langle Im(\mathbf{r}), Im(\mathbf{e}_1), Re(\mathbf{e}_2) \rangle \tag{10}$$

$$\langle \mathbf{u}, \mathbf{v}, \mathbf{w} \rangle = \sum_{n=1}^{d} [\mathbf{u}]_n [\mathbf{v}]_n [\mathbf{w}]_n \tag{11}$$

Since the asymmetry of this scoring function, namely $f_r(e_1, e_2) \neq f_r(e_2, e_1)$, ComplEx can effectively encode asymmetric relations (Trouillon et al., 2016). For calculating the attention, the $\mathbf{r}_{ht}$ in Equation 7 is defined via Equation 12, where $\odot$ represents the element-wise multiplication.

$$\mathbf{r}_{ht} = Re(\mathbf{e}_1) \odot Re(\mathbf{e}_2) + Im(\mathbf{e}_1) \odot Im(\mathbf{e}_2) \tag{12}$$

4.2 SimplE based Attention

Given a fact triplet (e_1, r, e_2), SimplE then encodes each entity $e \in \mathcal{E}$ into two vectors $\mathbf{h}_e$, $\mathbf{t}_e \in R^d$ and each relation $r \in \mathcal{R}$ into two vectors $\mathbf{v}_r$, $\mathbf{v}_{r^{-1}} \in R^d$ respectively, where d is the dimensionality of the embedding space. $\mathbf{h}_e$ captures the entity e's behaviour as the *head entity* of a fact triplet and $\mathbf{t}_e$ captures e's behaviour as the *tail entity*. $\mathbf{v}_r$ represents r in a fact triplet (e_1, r, e_2), while $\mathbf{v}_{r^{-1}}$ represents its inverse relation r^{-1} in the triplet (e_2, r^{-1}, e_1). The KG scoring function of SimplE for a fact triplet (e_1, r, e_2) is defined via Equation 13.

$$f_r(e_1, e_2) = \frac{1}{2}(\langle \mathbf{h}_{e_1}, \mathbf{v}_r, \mathbf{t}_{e_2} \rangle + \langle \mathbf{h}_{e_2}, \mathbf{v}_{r^{-1}}, \mathbf{t}_{e_1} \rangle) \tag{13}$$

Similar to the attention from ComplEx, the $\mathbf{r}_{ht}$ in Equation 7 is defined via Equation 14.

$$\mathbf{r}_{ht} = \frac{1}{2}(\mathbf{h}_{e_1} \odot \mathbf{h}_{e_2} + \mathbf{t}_{e_1} \odot \mathbf{t}_{e_2}) \tag{14}$$

4.3 SimplE_NER based Attention

The proposed end-to-end KGC model is based on SimplE, because SimplE outperforms several state-of-the-art models including ComplEx (Kazemi and Poole, 2018). The proposed model is illustrated in Figure 2. It includes ET classification part (below) and KG Scoring part (above). In ET classification part, a multi-layer perceptron (MLP) with two hidden layers are applied to identify ET based on word embedding of target entity. In KG Scoring part, *head entity* and *tail entity* along with their predicted ETs and their relation are projected into corresponding KG embeddings, which are then fed to a KG scoring function.

ET Classification Part. In this work, we use a MLP network to classify ET for *head entity* and *tail entity*. The architecture of our MLP network is as bellow:

$$\begin{aligned} \mathbf{h}_w &= \tanh(\mathbf{W}_{emb}^w \mathbf{x}^w), \\ \mathbf{h}_1 &= \text{sigmoid}(\mathbf{W}_1 \mathbf{h}_w + \mathbf{b}_1), \\ \mathbf{h}_2 &= \text{sigmoid}(\mathbf{W}_2 \mathbf{h}_1 + \mathbf{b}_2), \\ \mathbf{y} &= \text{sigmoid}(\mathbf{W}_{ET} \mathbf{h}_2 + \mathbf{b}_{ET}) \end{aligned} \tag{15}$$

where $\mathbf{W}_{emb}^w$ is a word embedding projection matrix, which is initialized by the pre-trained word

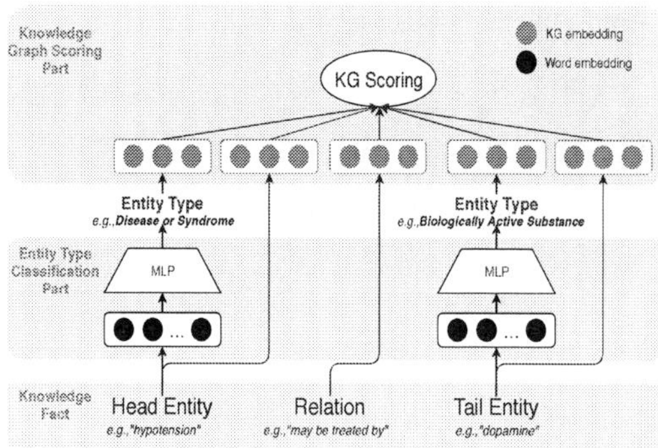

Figure 2: Overview of the proposed end-to-end KGC model.

embedding that is trained on Medline corpus via Gensim word2vec tool, $\mathbf{x}^w$ is a one-hot entity representation, $\mathbf{y}$ is the output vector containing the prediction probabilities of all target ETs. $\mathbf{W}_1$, $\mathbf{b}_1$, $\mathbf{W}_2$, $\mathbf{b}_2$, $\mathbf{W}_{ET}$ and $\mathbf{b}_{ET}$ are parameters to optimize.

KG Scoring Part. Given fact triplet and predicted ET pair ET_1 (for e_1) and ET_2 (for e_2), the proposed model project them into their corresponding KG embeddings namely $\mathbf{h}_{e_1}$, $\mathbf{t}_{e_1}$, $\mathbf{v}_r$, $\mathbf{v}_{r^{-1}}$, $\mathbf{h}_{e_2}$, $\mathbf{t}_{e_2}$, $\mathbf{h}_{ET_1}$, $\mathbf{t}_{ET_1}$, $\mathbf{h}_{ET_2}$ and $\mathbf{t}_{ET_2}$ respectively, where $\mathbf{h}_{ET_1}$ (or $\mathbf{t}_{ET_1}$) represents the KG embedding of ET for e_1 when e_1 acts as the *head entity* (or *tail entity*) in a fact triplet. The KG scoring function is defined via Equation 16. Since the proposed KGC model is build on SimplE, we apply Equation 14 to calculate $\mathbf{r}_{ht}$.

$$
\begin{aligned}
f_r(e_1, e_2) = \frac{1}{4}(&\langle \mathbf{h}_{e_1}, \mathbf{v}_r, \mathbf{t}_{e_2} \rangle \\
+&\langle \mathbf{h}_{e_2}, \mathbf{v}_{r^{-1}}, \mathbf{t}_{e_1} \rangle \\
+&\langle \mathbf{h}_{ET_1}, \mathbf{v}_r, \mathbf{t}_{ET_2} \rangle \\
+&\langle \mathbf{h}_{ET_2}, \mathbf{v}_{r^{-1}}, \mathbf{t}_{ET_1} \rangle)
\end{aligned}
\tag{16}
$$

5 Experiments

Our experiments aim to demonstrate that, (1) the base model proposed by (Han et al., 2018) is feasible for biomedical dataset, such as UMLS and Medline corpus, and (2) in order to improve the performance on the given biomedical dataset, it is necessary to extend the base model with other competitive KGC models, such as ComplEx and SimplE, and (3) the proposed end-to-end KGC model is effective for distantly supervised RE from biomedical dataset.

#Entity	#Relation	#Train	#Test
25,080	360	53,036	11,810

Table 1: Statistics of KG in this work.

5.1 Data

The biomedical datasets used for evaluation consist of biomedical knowledge graph and biomedical textual data, which will be detailed as follows.

Knowledge Graph. We choose the UMLS as the KG. UMLS is a large biomedical knowledge base developed at the U.S. National Library of Medicine. UMLS contains millions of biomedical concepts and relations between them. We follow (Wang et al., 2014), and only collect the fact triplet with RO relation category (RO stands for "has Relationship Other than synonymous, narrower, or broader"), which covers the interesting relations like *may_treat*, *my_prevent*, etc. From the UMLS 2018 release, we extract about 60 thousand such RO fact triplets (i.e., (e_1, r, e_2)) under the restriction that their entity pairs (i.e., e_1 and e_2) should coexist within a sentence in Medline corpus. They are then randomly divided into training and testing sets for KGC. Following (Weston et al., 2013), we keep high entity overlap between training and testing set, but zero fact triplet overlap. The statistics of the extracted KG is shown in Table 1. For training the ET Classification Part in Section 4.3, we also collect about 35 thousand entity-ET pairs (e.g., *heart rates*-`Clinical Attribute`) from the UMLS 2018 release.

Textual Data. Medline corpus is a collection of bimedical abstracts maintained by the National Library of Medicine. From the Medline corpus, by applying a string matching model [2], we extract $732,771$ sentences that contain the entity pairs (i.e., e_1 and e_2) in the KG mentioned above as our textual data, in which $592,605$ sentences are for training and $140,166$ sentences for testing. For identifying the NA relation, besides the "related" sentences, we also extract the "unrelated" sentences based on a closed world assumption: pairs of entities not listed in the KG are regarded to have NA relation and sentences containing them considered to be the "unrelated" sentences. By this way, we extract $1,738,801$ "unrelated" sentences for the training data, and $431,212$ "unrelated" sentences for the testing data. Table 2 presents some

---

[2] We adopt the NER model that is available at `https://github.com/mpuig/spacy-lookup`.

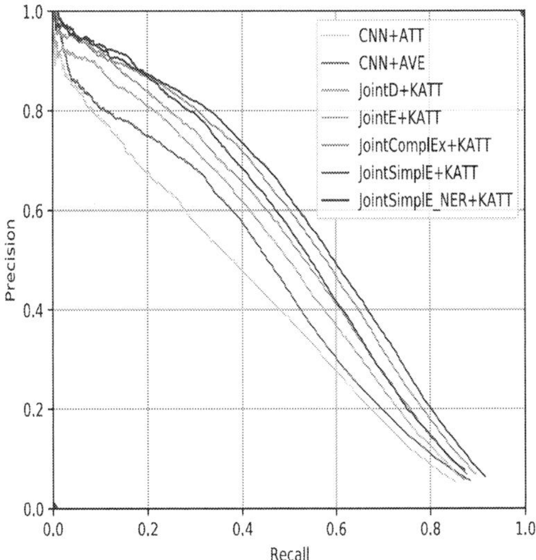

Figure 3: Aggregate precision/recall curves for different RE models.

sample sentences in the training data.

5.2 Parameter Settings

We base our work on (Han et al., 2018) and extend their implementation available at `https://github.com/thunlp/JointNRE`, and thus adopt identical optimization process. We use the default settings of parameters [3] provided by the base model. Since we address the distantly supervised RE in biomedical domain, we use the Medline corpus to train the domain specific word embedding projection matrix $\mathbf{W}_{emb}^{w}$.

5.3 Result and Discussion

(Han et al., 2018) evaluates the base model on non-scientific dataset. In this work, we firstly plan to assess its feasibility on scientific dataset, and secondly, to investigate the effectiveness of our extensions, which is discussed in Section 4, with respect to enhancing the distantly supervised RE from scientific dataset.

Relation Extraction We follow (Mintz et al., 2009; Weston et al., 2013; Lin et al., 2016; Han et al., 2018) and conduct the held-out evaluation, in which the model for distantly supervised RE is evaluated by comparing the fact triplets identified from textual data (i.e., the bag of sentences containing the target entity pairs) with those in

KG. We report precision-recall curves and Precision@N (P@N) as well in our evaluation.

The precision-recall curves are shown in Figure 3, where "JointD+KATT" and "JointE+KATT" represent the RE model with the KG-based attention obtained from Prob-TransD and Prob-TransE respectively, which are our base models and trained on both KG and textual data. Similarly, "JointComplEx+KATT", "JointSimplE+KATT" and "JointSimplE_NER+KATT" represent the RE model with the KG-based attention obtained from ComplEx, SimplE and SimplE_NER respectively, which are our extensions. "CNN+AVE" and "CNN+ATT" represent the RE model with average attention and relation vector based attention (Lin et al., 2016) respectively, which are not joint models and only trained on textual data. The results show that:

(1) All RE models with KG-based attention, such as "JointE+KATT", outperform those models without it, such as "CNN+ATT". This observation is in line with (Han et al., 2018). This demonstrates that not just for non-scientific dataset , jointly training a KGC model with a RE model is also an effective approach to improve the performance of distantly supervised RE for biomedical dataset. In other words, the outperformance proves the feasibility of the base model proposed by (Han et al., 2018) on biomedical dataset. The comparison between (Han et al., 2018)'s results on non-scientific dataset and ours on scientific dataset also indicates that the performance of base model could differ according to the dataset. Specifically, on scientific dataset, "JointE+KATT" performs better than "JointD+KATT" but in non-scientific dataset the latter outperforms the former.

(2) Our extended models, "JointComplEx+KATT", "JointSimplE+KATT" and "JointSimplE_NER+KATT", achieve better precision than the base model over the major range of recall. It could be attributed to their better capability of modeling asymmetric relations (e.g., may_treat and $may\_prevent$), because their KG scoring functions are asymmetry (i.e., $f_r(e_1, e_2) \neq f_r(e_2, e_1)$). The superior performance indicates the necessity of our extensions on the base model. Specifically, given the frequently used biomedical dataset, UMLS and Medline corpus, it would be an effective method to switch the translational distance models, such as TransE and TransD, with the semantic matching models,

---

[3]As a preliminary study, we only adopt the default hyperparameters, but we will tune them in the furture.

Fact Triplet	Textual Data
(insulin, gene_plays_role_in_process, lipid_metabolism)	s_1 : *It is unknown whether short - term angiotensin_receptor blocker therapy can improve glucose and lipid_metabolism$_{e_2}$ in insulin$_{e_1}$ - resistant subjects.* s_2 : *Adipocyte lipid_metabolism$_{e_2}$ is primarily regulated by insulin$_{e_1}$ and the catecholamines norepinephrine and epinephrine.* s_3 : ...
(insulin, NA, TPA)	s_1 : *M wortmannin resulted in 80% and 20% decreases of glucose uptake stimulated by insulin$_{e_1}$ and TPA$_{e_2}$, respectively.* s_2 : *The effects of insulin$_{e_1}$, IGF1 and TPA$_{e_2}$ were also observed in the presence of cycloheximide.* s_3 : ...

Table 2: Examples of textual data extracted from Medline corpus.

such as ComplEx and SimplE, for increasing the performance of distantly supervised RE. The effect of different KGC models on the distantly supervised RE will be discussed later.

(3) The model enhanced by our proposed KGC model, "JointSimplE_NER+KATT", achieves the highest precision over almost entire range of recall compared with the models that apply the existing KGC models. This proves the effectiveness of our proposed KGC model for the distantly supervised RE. Additionally, different from the exiting KGC models, the proposed end-to-end KGC model is capable of identifying ET information from word embedding of target entity. This indicates that the incorporation of semantic information of entity, such as ET, is a promising approach for enhancing the base model.

Effect of KGC on RE. (Han et al., 2018) indicates that KGC models could affect the performance of distantly supervised RE. For investigating the influence of KGC models on our specific RE task, we compare their link prediction results on our KG with their corresponding Precision@N (P@N) results on our RE task. Link prediction is the task that predicts *tail entity t* given both *head entity h* and *relation r*, e.g., $(h, r, *)$, or predict *head entity h* given $(*, r, t)$. We report the mean reciprocal rank (MRR) and mean Hit@N scores for evaluating the KGC models. MRR is defined as: $MRR = \frac{1}{2*|tt|} \sum_{(h,r,t)\in tt}(\frac{1}{rank_h} + \frac{1}{rank_t})$, where tt represents the test triplets. Hit@N is the proportion of the correctly predicted entities (h or t) in top N ranked entities. Table 3 and Table 4 represent the RE precision@N and link prediction results respectively. This comparison indicates that given a biomedical dataset, the performance of a KGC model on the link prediction task could predict its effectiveness on its corresponding distantly

supervised RE task. This observation also instruct us how to select the best KGC model for the base model. In addition, Table 3 and Table 4 indicate that ET is not only effective for distantly supervised RE task, but also for KGC task, and this observation will inspire us to explore other useful semantic feature of entity, such as the definition of entity, for our task.

Model	P@2k	P@4k	P@6k	Mean
JointE+KATT	0.876	0.786	0.698	0.786
JointD+KATT	0.848	0.725	0.528	0.700
JointComplEx+KATT	0.892	0.819	0.741	0.817
JointSimplE+KATT	0.900	0.808	0.721	0.809
JointSimplE_NER+KATT	**0.913**	**0.829**	**0.753**	**0.831**

Table 3: P@N for different RE models, where k=1000.

Model	MRR		Hit@		
	Raw	Filter	1	3	10
TransE	0.156	0.200	0.113	0.244	0.356
TransD	0.138	0.149	0.098	0.160	0.245
ComplEx	0.278	0.457	0.380	0.507	0.587
SimplE	0.273	0.455	0.368	0.516	0.598
SimplE_NER	**0.339**	**0.538**	**0.473**	**0.578**	**0.651**

Table 4: Link prediction results for different KGC models.

6 Conclusion and Future Work

In this work, we tackle the task of distantly supervised RE from biomedical publications. To this end, we apply the strong joint framework proposed by (Han et al., 2018) as the base model. For enhancing its performance on our specific task, we extend the base model with other competitive KGC models. What is more, we also propose a new end-to-end KGC model, which incorporates word embedding based entity type information into a sate-of-the-art KGC model. Experimental results not only show the feasibility of the base model on the biomedical domain, but also indicate the effectiveness of our extensions. Our extended model achieves significant and consistent improvements on the biomedical dataset as compared with baselines. Since the semantic information of target entity, such as ET information, is effective for our task, in the future, we will explore other useful semantic features, such as the definition of target entity and fact triplet chain between entities (e.g., cancer→disease_has_associated_gene→ Ku86→gene_plays_role_in_process→NHEJ), for our task.

Acknowledgement

This work was supported by JST CREST Grant Number JPMJCR1513, Japan and KAKENHI Grant Number 16H06614.

References

Waleed Ammar, Matthew Peters, Chandra Bhagavatula, and Russell Power. 2017. The ai2 system at semeval-2017 task 10 (scienceie): semi-supervised end-to-end entity and relation extraction. In *Proceedings of the 11th International Workshop on Semantic Evaluation (SemEval-2017)*, pages 592–596.

Kurt Bollacker, Colin Evans, Praveen Paritosh, Tim Sturge, and Jamie Taylor. 2008. Freebase: a collaboratively created graph database for structuring human knowledge. In *Proceedings of the 2008 ACM SIGMOD international conference on Management of data*, pages 1247–1250. AcM.

Antoine Bordes, Nicolas Usunier, Alberto Garcia-Duran, Jason Weston, and Oksana Yakhnenko. 2013. Translating embeddings for modeling multi-relational data. In *Advances in neural information processing systems*, pages 2787–2795.

Jinghang Gu, Fuqing Sun, Longhua Qian, and Guodong Zhou. 2017. Chemical-induced disease relation extraction via convolutional neural network. *Database*, 2017.

Gus Hahn-Powell, Dane Bell, Marco A Valenzuela-Escárcega, and Mihai Surdeanu. 2016. This before that: Causal precedence in the biomedical domain. *arXiv preprint arXiv:1606.08089*.

Xu Han, Zhiyuan Liu, and Maosong Sun. 2018. Neural knowledge acquisition via mutual attention between knowledge graph and text. In *Thirty-Second AAAI Conference on Artificial Intelligence*.

Raphael Hoffmann, Congle Zhang, Xiao Ling, Luke Zettlemoyer, and Daniel S Weld. 2011. Knowledge-based weak supervision for information extraction of overlapping relations. In *Proceedings of the 49th Annual Meeting of the Association for Computational Linguistics: Human Language Technologies-Volume 1*, pages 541–550. Association for Computational Linguistics.

Guoliang Ji, Shizhu He, Liheng Xu, Kang Liu, and Jun Zhao. 2015. Knowledge graph embedding via dynamic mapping matrix. In *Proceedings of the 53rd Annual Meeting of the Association for Computational Linguistics and the 7th International Joint Conference on Natural Language Processing (Volume 1: Long Papers)*, volume 1, pages 687–696.

Seyed Mehran Kazemi and David Poole. 2018. Simple embedding for link prediction in knowledge graphs. In *Advances in Neural Information Processing Systems*, pages 4289–4300.

Jens Lehmann, Robert Isele, Max Jakob, Anja Jentzsch, Dimitris Kontokostas, Pablo N Mendes, Sebastian Hellmann, Mohamed Morsey, Patrick Van Kleef, Sören Auer, et al. 2015. Dbpedia–a large-scale, multilingual knowledge base extracted from wikipedia. *Semantic Web*, 6(2):167–195.

Yankai Lin, Shiqi Shen, Zhiyuan Liu, Huanbo Luan, and Maosong Sun. 2016. Neural relation extraction with selective attention over instances. In *Proceedings of the 54th Annual Meeting of the Association for Computational Linguistics (Volume 1: Long Papers)*, volume 1, pages 2124–2133.

Tomas Mikolov, Ilya Sutskever, Kai Chen, Greg S Corrado, and Jeff Dean. 2013. Distributed representations of words and phrases and their compositionality. In *Advances in neural information processing systems*, pages 3111–3119.

Mike Mintz, Steven Bills, Rion Snow, and Dan Jurafsky. 2009. Distant supervision for relation extraction without labeled data. In *Proceedings of the Joint Conference of the 47th Annual Meeting of the ACL and the 4th International Joint Conference on Natural Language Processing of the AFNLP: Volume 2-Volume 2*, pages 1003–1011. Association for Computational Linguistics.

Makoto Miwa and Mohit Bansal. 2016. End-to-end relation extraction using lstms on sequences and tree structures. *arXiv preprint arXiv:1601.00770*.

Randall Munroe. 2013. The rise of open access. *Science*, 342(6154):58–59.

Sebastian Riedel, Limin Yao, and Andrew McCallum. 2010. Modeling relations and their mentions without labeled text. In *Joint European Conference on Machine Learning and Knowledge Discovery in Databases*, pages 148–163. Springer.

Cicero Nogueira dos Santos, Bing Xiang, and Bowen Zhou. 2015. Classifying relations by ranking with convolutional neural networks. *arXiv preprint arXiv:1504.06580*.

Théo Trouillon, Johannes Welbl, Sebastian Riedel, Éric Gaussier, and Guillaume Bouchard. 2016. Complex embeddings for simple link prediction. In *International Conference on Machine Learning*, pages 2071–2080.

Quan Wang, Zhendong Mao, Bin Wang, and Li Guo. 2017. Knowledge graph embedding: A survey of approaches and applications. *IEEE Transactions on Knowledge and Data Engineering*, 29(12):2724–2743.

Zhen Wang, Jianwen Zhang, Jianlin Feng, and Zheng Chen. 2014. Knowledge graph embedding by translating on hyperplanes. In *AAAI*, volume 14, pages 1112–1119.

Jason Weston, Antoine Bordes, Oksana Yakhnenko, and Nicolas Usunier. 2013. Connecting language and knowledge bases with embedding models for relation extraction. *arXiv preprint arXiv:1307.7973*.

Ruobing Xie, Zhiyuan Liu, and Maosong Sun. 2016. Representation learning of knowledge graphs with hierarchical types. In *IJCAI*, pages 2965–2971.

Kun Xu, Yansong Feng, Songfang Huang, and Dongyan Zhao. 2015. Semantic relation classification via convolutional neural networks with simple negative sampling. *arXiv preprint arXiv:1506.07650*.

Daojian Zeng, Kang Liu, Yubo Chen, and Jun Zhao. 2015. Distant supervision for relation extraction via piecewise convolutional neural networks. In *Proceedings of the 2015 Conference on Empirical Methods in Natural Language Processing*, pages 1753–1762.

Daojian Zeng, Kang Liu, Siwei Lai, Guangyou Zhou, Jun Zhao, et al. 2014. Relation classification via convolutional deep neural network. In *COLING*, pages 2335–2344.

Dongxu Zhang and Dong Wang. 2015. Relation classification via recurrent neural network. *arXiv preprint arXiv:1508.01006*.

Peng Zhou, Wei Shi, Jun Tian, Zhenyu Qi, Bingchen Li, Hongwei Hao, and Bo Xu. 2016. Attention-based bidirectional long short-term memory networks for relation classification. In *Proceedings of the 54th Annual Meeting of the Association for Computational Linguistics (Volume 2: Short Papers)*, volume 2, pages 207–212.

Scalable, Semi-Supervised Extraction of Structured Information from Scientific Literature

Kritika Agrawal, Aakash Mittal, Vikram Pudi
Data Sciences and Analytics Center, Kohli Center on Intelligent Systems
IIIT, Hyderabad, India
{kritika.agrawal@research.,aakash.mittal@students.,vikram@}iiit.ac.in

Abstract

As scientific communities grow and evolve, there is a high demand for improved methods for finding relevant papers, comparing papers on similar topics and studying trends in the research community. All these tasks involve the common problem of extracting structured information from scientific articles. In this paper, we propose a novel, scalable, semi-supervised method for extracting relevant structured information from the vast available raw scientific literature. We extract the fundamental concepts of *aim, method* and *result* from scientific articles and use them to construct a knowledge graph. Our algorithm makes use of domain-based word embedding and the bootstrap framework. Our experiments show the domain independence of our algorithm and that our system achieves precision and recall comparable to the state of the art. We also show the research trends of two distinct communities - computational linguistics and computer vision.

1 Introduction

With the tremendous amount of research publications available online, there is an increasing demand to automatically process this information to facilitate easy navigation through this enormous literature for researchers. Whenever researchers start working on a problem, they are interested to know if the problem has been solved previously, methods used to solve this problem, the importance of the problem and the applications of that problem. This leads to the requirement of finding automatic ways of extracting such structured information from the vast available raw scientific literature which can help summarize the research paper as well as the research community and can help in finding relevant papers. Organizing scientific information into structured knowledge bases requires information extraction (IE) about scientific entities and their relationships. However, the challenges associated with scientific information extraction are greater than for a general domain. General methods of information extraction cannot be applied to research papers due to their semi-structured nature and also the new and unique terminologies used in them. Secondly, annotation of scientific text requires domain expertise which makes annotation costly and limits resources.

There is a considerable amount of previous and ongoing work in this direction, starting from keyword extraction (Kim et al., 2010) (Gollapalli and Caragea, 2014) and textual summarization (Jaidka et al., 2018). Other research has focused on unsupervised approaches such as bootstrapping (Tsai et al., 2013)(Gupta and Manning, 2011), where they introduced hand-designed templates to extract scientific keyphrases and categorize them into different concepts, and then more templates are added automatically through bootstrapping. Hand-designed templates limit their generalization to all the different domains present within the scientific literature. A recent challenge on Scientific Information Extraction (ScienceIE) (Augenstein et al., 2017) provided a dataset consisting of 500 scientific paragraphs with keyphrase annotations for three categories: TASK, PROCESS, MATERIAL across three scientific domains, Computer Science, Material Science, and Physics. This invited many supervised and semi-supervised techniques in this field. Although all these techniques can help extract important concepts of a research paper in a particular domain, we need more general and scalable methods which can summarize the complete research community.

In this work, we propose a new technique to extract key concepts from the research publications. Our main insight is that a paper cites another paper either for its aim, or method, or result. Therefore, key contribution of paper in the research community can be best summarized by its aim, the method used to solve the problem and

Proceedings of the Workshop on Extracting Structured Knowledge from Scientific Publications, pages 11–20
Minneapolis, USA, June 6, 2019. ©2019 Association for Computational Linguistics

the final result. We define these concepts as:

Aim: Target or primary focus of the paper.

Method: Techniques used to achieve the aim.

Result: well-defined output of the experiments or contribution which can be directly used by the research community.

Example: "The support-vector network (*Result*) is a new learning machine for two-group classification (*Aim*) problems. The machine conceptually implements the following idea: input vectors are non-linearly mapped to a very high-dimension feature space (*Method*). In this feature space, a linear decision surface is constructed."

We extract these concepts from Title, Abstract and Citation Contexts of a research paper. These sections can be accurately automatically extracted from research papers. Title and Abstract work as a short and to the point summary of work done in the paper. They are an essential place to find the exact phrases for these concepts without the introduction of too much noise. Citation context is the text around the citation marker. This text serves as "micro summaries" of a cited paper and phrases in this text are important candidates for aim, method or result of the cited paper. We combine data mining and natural language techniques to solve the problem scalably in a semi-supervised manner. Graph representations like knowledge graph that link the information of a large body of publications can reveal patterns and lead to the discovery of new information that would not be apparent from the analysis of just one publication. Analysis on top of these representations can lead to new scientific insights and discovery of trends in a research area. They can also facilitate some other tasks like assigning reviewers, recommending relevant papers or improving scientific search engines. Therefore, we propose to build graphical representation by extracting phrases representing the concepts *Aim*, *Method* and *Result* from scientific publications. We introduce these phrases as additional nodes and connect them to their corresponding paper nodes in the citation graph. We argue that the citation network is an integral part of scientific knowledge graph and the proposed representation can adequately summarize the research community. Proposed graph is shown in Figure 1.

Contributions: Our key contributions are:
(i) We propose a novel, scalable, semi-supervised and domain-independent method for extracting concepts, *aim*, *method* and *result* from the vast available raw scientific literature by using domain-based word embeddings and data mining techniques. Our approach also takes Citation Context into account apart from Title and Abstract on which most of the work relied till now. (ii) We experimentally validate our approach and show statistically significant improvements over existing state-of-the-art models. (iii) We show how the extracted concepts and the available citation graph can be used to represent the research community as a knowledge graph. (iv) We demonstrate our method on a large multi-domain dataset built with the help of DBLP citation network. Our dataset consists of 332,793 papers and 1,508,560 links between them. (v) We present a case study on the computational linguistics community and computer vision community using the three concepts extracted from its articles, for verifying the results of our system and for showing domain independence of our approach.

Our research background, hypothesis, and motivation were presented in this section. In the following section, we describe proposed approach in detail. Finally, we present our datasets, experiments, and results and briefly summarize state-of-the-art approaches before concluding the paper.

2 Approach

2.1 Concept Extraction

Problem Definition: Given a target document d, the objective of the concept extraction task is to extract a list of words or phrases which best represent the aim, method and result of document d.

Prior work has solved the problem of extracting keyphrases and relations between them as a sequence labelling task. However, due to the non-availability of large annotated data for this purpose

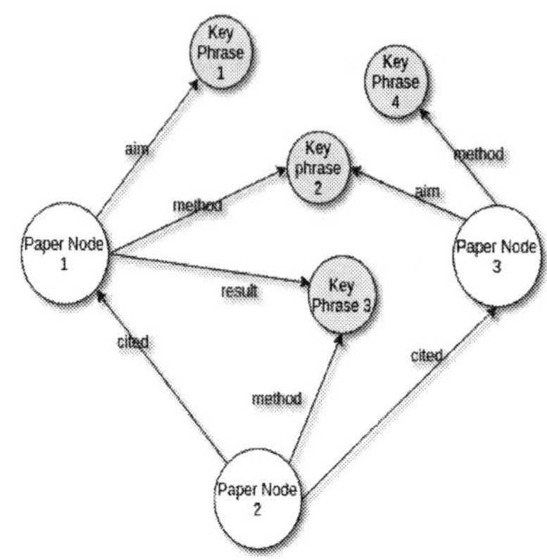

Figure 1: Structure of proposed Representation

limits this approach. Also this approach does not take advantage of the fact that more than 96 percent of phrases that form aim, method and result are noun phrases (Augenstein et al., 2017). Since we already have a defined set of candidates for the key phrases, we attempt this problem as multiclass classification problem. Given a document, we classify its phrases as *Aim, Method, Result*. Our approach is built on the observation that the semantics of the sentence of document d containing a phrase belonging to any of the concept type is similar across research papers. To capture this semantic similarity, we use k nearest neighbour classifier on top of state-of-the-art (Devlin et al., 2018) domain based word embeddings. We start by extracting features from a small set of annotated examples and used bootstrapping (Gupta and Manning, 2014) for extracting new features from unlabeled dataset. Figure 2 shows our pipeline.

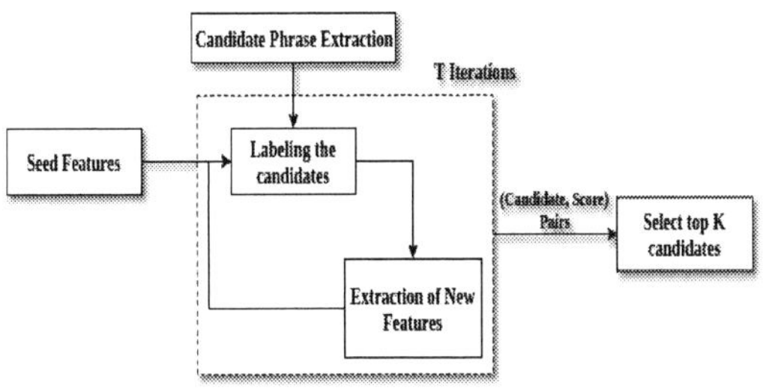

Figure 2: Proposed Method

Following are some of the terminologies which will be used throughout the paper that follows:

- *Candidate phrases*: Phrases present in the target document d which will be considered for labeling.
- *Concept mention*: Phrases labeled as either aim, method or Result in the labeled dataset.
- *Parent sentence of a phrase p*: The original sentence in target document to which the candidate phrase/concept mention p belongs to.
- *Left context phrase(S,p)*: The part of the parent sentence S before the occurrence of the candidate phrase p or concept mention.
- *Right context phrase(S,p)*: The part of the parent sentence S after the occurrence of the candidate phrase p or concept mention.
- *Left Context Vectors(p)*: Vector representations of left context phrase p.
- *Right Context Vectors(p)*: Vector representations of right context phrase p.
- *Feature Vectors*: Tuple of Left and Right Context Vectors which is being used as features to label candidate phrases.

- *Feature Score*: Each feature vector has an associated feature score between 0 and 1 that represents the confidence of it being a representative of the class. Seed features have a feature score of 1.
- *Support Score of candidate phrase p for class c*: Every phrase is assigned a support score for all classes that represents the confidence that the phrase belongs to that class.

Seed Feature Extraction: In this step, we extract features for each of the concept type using the small set of annotated examples. For each concept mention in the annotated examples, we construct left context vector *lcv* and right context vector *rcv*. These *lcv* and *rcv* then form part of the features for the class to which concept mention belongs to. Phrase embeddings are generated using pre-trained BERT model (Devlin et al., 2018) fine-tuned on DBLP research papers dataset. Details of BERT training and datasets used for seed feature extraction are given in the Experiments Section.

Candidate Phrase Extraction: To limit the search space of phrases, we propose to use noun phrases present in the Title and Abstract of document d as candidate phrases. For citation contexts, named entities form a better set of candidates as shown by (Ganguly and Pudi, 2016). However different named entities can be linked to different papers cited in the same citation context. So it becomes essential to first identify which entity e corresponds to which cited paper cp and then use the proposed algorithm to classify e as aim/method/result for the corresponding paper cp. For the above purpose, we use entity-citation linking algorithm (Ganguly and Pudi, 2016). The matching function iterates over entities and citations to get their closeness score. After the scoring step, a two-step pruning is performed. It first takes all the citations and keeps a list of the closest entity per citation. Then it takes the remaining entities and keeps only the closest citations per entity. Finally, we get a list of tuples where each element contains a unique entity matched with its citation. Only the entities which are present in this list of tuples are considered as candidate phrases.

Labeling Candidate Phrases: For labeling candidates in iteration i, we use k-NN. The algorithm for labeling candidate phrases is presented in Algorithm 1.

Algorithm 1: Label Candidate Phrases

1. For each sentence s in document d in the dataset, $p \leftarrow$ unlabeled Phrase in sentence s.

2. Let *lcv* be the left context vector and *rcv* be the right context vector corresponding to phrase p in sentence s.

3. Find nearest neigbours of lcv and rcv from the feature vectors that are atmax distance r. Let the nearest neigbours corresponding to lcv be *lnn or left nearest neighbours* and rcv be *rnn or right nearest neighbours*.

4. If the size of both *lnn* and *rnn* is less than the minimum number of neighbours required for classification k then the phrase can not be labeled in this iteration and we move to the next phrase.

5. Else we take k nearest neighbours for both the lcv and rcv and the support score of the phrase for class c is calculated as follows :
$N = \{n | n \in \text{Top k Neighbours of } lcv \text{ or } rcv$
$\text{and } label(n) = c \}$

$$supportScore(p, c) = \sum_{n \in N} featureScore(n)$$

6. Then the predicted class for phrase p is $\arg\max_{c} supportScore(p, c)$.

Finally after T iterations, unlabeled candidate phrases are discarded.

Extraction of new features: For each phrase p assigned class c in any of the iterations, we generate context vectors lcv and rcv. We define the feature score corresponding to the context vectors of phrase p labeled as class c as:

$$featureScore(p) = \frac{supprtScore(p, c)}{\sum_{c'} supportScore(p, c')}$$

For each class, the context vectors are sorted based on their feature score and top 5000 are taken as feature vectors.

Final Selection: For each document, we take top t phrases (based on their *supportScore*) for each class as the final output of our system.

2.2 Graph Construction

Graph definition: We build a graphical representation by using the extracted concepts and citation graph. Our graph has the following types of nodes and edges:

Paper nodes: These are the original paper nodes in the citation graph. Each paper node has metadata related to the paper like dblp id, title, authors, conference, year of publication.

Entity nodes: These nodes are the phrases extracted in the concept extraction step.

Cited_by relation: A cited_by relation is defined between paper nodes p_i and p_j if paper p_i has cited p_j.

Aim relation: Aim relation is defined between a paper node p_i and entity node e_i if e_i was extracted as aim concept for p_i.

Method relation: A method relation is defined between a paper node p_i and entity node e_i if e_i was extracted as method concept for p_i.

Result relation: A result relation is defined between a paper node p_i and entity node e_i if e_i was extracted as a result concept for p_i.

Construction of Graph: A major challenge in the construction of graph using phrases extracted in concept extraction step is merging of phrases with the same meaning. For the purpose of entity node merging, we do the following:

1. We group the papers according to the conference in which they were published. Then $\forall$ papers in the same group, we cluster their extracted phrases by running DBSCAN (Ester et al., 1996) over vector space representations of these phrases. The clusters are created based on lexical similarity which is captured by cosine distance between phrase embeddings. The intuition behind clustering phrases conference wise is that the research papers in a conference have same domain and thus phrases with high lexical similarity belonging to a particular conference are much more likely to mean the same as compared to phrases across conferences. This helps to avoid error as in the example : 'real time intrusion detection' in security domain and 'real time object detection' in computer vision domain are very different from each other but they may be clustered together by DBSCAN algorithm based on lexical similarity if DBSCAN is run on all the papers in the dataset at once.

2. Clusters merging across conferences: A cluster i belonging to conference c_1 and a cluster j belonging to conference c_2 are merged if they have any common phrase. This is done to capture the fact that there can be more than one conference

on same domain and hence some of their clusters should be merged if they correspond to same term or phrase. For example, both NAACL and ACL have papers on machine translation and therefore the individual clusters of these conferences corresponding to machine translation should be merged.

Finally we get clusters such that phrases in each cluster have the same meaning. We add only one entity node to the graph for each cluster. We define the relation type between a paper node and an entity node based on the label of the entity (phrase inside the entity node) for the corresponding paper as identified in Concept Extraction step.

3 Experimental Setup

Dataset Creation: All the experiments were conducted on DBLP Citation Network (version 7) dataset. This dataset is an extensive collection of computer science papers. DBLP only provides citation-link information, abstract, and paper titles. For the full text of these papers, we use the same dataset as have been used by (Ganguly and Pudi, 2017). This dataset is partly noisy with some duplicate paper information, and there is a lack of unique one-to-one mapping from the DBLP paper ids to the actual text of that paper. During the creation of our final dataset, we either pruned out ambiguous papers or manually resolved the conflicts. We came up with a final set of 465,355 papers from the DBLP corpus for which we have full text available. Since we need papers that are connected via citation relations, we prune our dataset by taking only the largest connected component in the citation network while considering the links to be bidirectional. We get 332,793 papers having 1,508,560 citation links. For extraction of citation context, we used Parscit (Prasad et al., 2018). For the papers for which abstract was not available in the DBLP dataset, we use the one extracted by Parscit.

Phrase embeddings: For vector representation of a phrase, we use BERT: Pre-training of Deep Bidirectional Transformers for Language Understanding as proposed in (Devlin et al., 2018). We use the pre-trained model BERT-Base, Uncased: 12-layer, 768-hidden, 12-heads, 110M parameters available publically. We fine tune the model on our DBLP research paper dataset. Complete text of papers after cleaning has been used for the purpose of fine tuning. The model is fined tuned on total of 20970300 sentences with max sequence length as 128 and learning rate as 2×10^{-5}. For generating the phrase embedding we use second last layer as the pooling layer with pooling strategy as reduced mean.

Concept Extraction: (a) For the purpose of seed feature generation we use the following two publicly available datasets :

(i) SemEval 2017 Task 10 dataset (Augenstein et al., 2017): It contains 500 scientific paragraphs from physics, material science and computer science domain, each marked with keyphrases and each keyphrase is labelled as TASK, PROCESS and MATERIAL. The concepts of TASK and PROCESS in this dataset closely relates to our definition of AIM and METHOD. This complete dataset is used for seed feature extraction.

(ii) Gupta and Manning(2011) introduced a dataset of titles and abstracts of 474 research publications from ACL Anthology annotated with phrases corresponding to FOCUS, TECHNIQUE and DOMAIN. Their definitions of FOCUS and TECHNIQUE closely relate to our definitions of AIM and METHOD respectively. We divided this data into two parts- one is used as training data for seed features extraction having 277 papers and another as test data for evaluation purposes having 197 papers.

These two datasets helped to build seed features for AIM and METHOD category. We removed the papers from SemEval dataset which overlapped with (Gupta and Manning, 2011).

For RESULT, we manually annotated titles and abstracts of 100 research publications in computer science domain.

(b) While generating vector encoding for context phrases, we limit the length of the context phrase to 25 in-order to handle very long sentences. We used cosine distance to measure distance between vector representation of the phrases.

(c) It may be possible that there are more than one concept mention in a sentence. To nullify the effect of other concept mentions, we generated the seed features list in two ways:

- Take the left context phrase and right context phrase and generate their vector representation. This is called as *unmasked feature list*.

- We mask the other candidate phrases C in the left and right context phrase of candidate c_i

k	r	t	f1 score	precision	recall
30	0.65	3	**40.66**	46.04	**36.41**
60	0.65	3	40.47	**52.60**	32.88
40	0.65	3	40.38	48.65	34.51
40	0.60	4	40.06	47.12	34.84
30	0.75	4	38.38	41.95	35.37

Table 1: f1, precision & recall score for AIM concept

k	r	t	f1 score	precision	recall
40	0.85	20	**32.58**	22.65	58.1
30	0.75	17	30.81	21.12	56.89
30	0.90	14	30.87	**23.78**	44
30	0.80	25	31.16	20.72	**62.77**
30	0.65	15	30.69	21.35	54.6

Table 2: f1, precision & recall score for METHOD concept

Approach	f1 score	precision	recall
GM (2011)	30.5	46.7	36.9
(Tsai et al., 2013)	48.2	48.8	48.5
Our Approach	32.58	22.65	**58.1**

Table 3: Comparison with state-of-the-art for METHOD Concept

Approach	f1 score	precision	recall
(Tsai et al., 2013)	8.26	31.37	4.761
Our Approach	**40.66**	46.04	**36.41**

Table 4: Comparison with state-of-the-art for AIM Concept on DBLP dataset

Approach	f1 score	precision	recall
(Tsai et al., 2013)	18.0	50.70	10.94
Our Approach	**32.58**	22.65	58.1

Table 5: Comparison with state-of-the-art for Method Concept on DBLP dataset

before generating their embedding. This is called as *masked feature list*.

Experiments were done for masked and unmasked feature lists separately.

(d) As number of phrases added per iteration decreased substantially after iteration 5, we ran only 5 iterations of bootstrapping algorithm for all the experiments.

(e) We experimented with different values of distance r and k. We observed that in general precision increases with increase in value of k and recall increases with decrease in value of r.

Evaluation: For evaluating our results, we use the labeled dataset made available by (Gupta and Manning, 2011). We used 197 out of 474 papers for evaluation purpose. We calculate precision, recall and f1 score for each class. However, as *Result* phrases were not annotated in that dataset, we could evaluate only for *Aim* and *Method*. We compare our proposed approach with (Tsai et al., 2013) which ran the bootstrapping algorithm for a similar problem but used n-gram based features. They reported results for ACL Anthopology Network(AAN) Corpus (Radev et al., 2013). We ran their algorithm on our dataset with parameter tuning as mentioned by them.

4 Results and Discussion

4.1 Concept Extraction

We got the best results for parameter values, $r = 0.65$ and $k = 60$. Our bootstrapping algorithm gave output for 332,242 out of 332,793 papers. In Table 1, we report the top five scores for *Aim* for different parameters. Top ten scores for both aim and method concept were given by unmasked feature list. Therefore mask feature list results have not been shown. In Table 2 we report the top five scores for *Method* on different parameters. Table 3 and 4 compares our scores with that of (Gupta and Manning, 2011) and (Tsai et al., 2013). Table 5 compares our scores with the score computed for (Tsai et al., 2013) approach on our dataset.

Our proposed algorithm was able to extract phrases from scientific articles in a large dataset in semi-supervised manner with f1 score comparable to the state-of-the-art. Our f1 score was lower as compared to (Gupta and Manning, 2011) (Tsai et al., 2013). However, our recall was consistently higher. Our precision was perhaps low as we were considering only the noun phrases whereas such limitation was not there while annotating the test corpus. They (Gupta and Manning, 2011) (Tsai et al., 2013) used hand crafted features for AAN Corpus whereas our features were extracted algorithmically starting from a small annotated dataset containing multiple domains such as physics, material science and computer science. Table 5 shows the scalability of our approach. Tsai et al. (2013) bootstrapping algorithm could not give a decent score when ran on our multi-domain dataset because phrases could not be extracted for most of the papers.

4.2 Graph Construction

Total number of unique phrases produced by the proposed algorithm are 565,031. Using DB-SCAN we form 63,638 clusters having 266,015 phrases. Our final graph contains 332,242 paper nodes, 362654 entity nodes, 483899 aim relations, 982396 relations and 661 result relations. We store our graph in Neo4j database (Webber and Robinson, 2018). A small sample from our constructed graph is shown in figure 3. We can see that result relations are quite few as compared to method and aim relations. This is mainly because of less number of seed features for Result due to less annotated data as compared to Aim and Method.

The constructed graph can summarize the research community in the following way:

(i) All the papers on a particular topic can be accessed by just finding the entity node corresponding to the topic in the graph. The associated papers can also be differentiated on the basis of whether the topic appears as aim or method or result in the paper. This can also help in academic search and recommendation.

(ii) A field can be summarized by finding all the *methods* used in the field and applications of field by finding all the *aims* where the field has been used as *method*.

(iii) Trend Analysis, conference proceedings summarization, or summarization of a particular author's work can be done using the meta data in the paper node.

Neo4j provides interface for all kind of queries required for the above applications. The queries are out of scope of this paper.

5 Trend Analysis

We studied the field of computational linguistics and computer vision.

Computational Linguistics: We studied the growth and decline of following topics on the basis of relative number of papers published on each topic over a period of years: *summarization, word sense disambiguation* and *machine translation*. Papers are included from NAACL and ACL conferences from 1990 to 2012. Figure 4 and 6 show an example of trends as extracted from our constructed knowledge graph. Figure 6 shows transition of a topic from aim to method concept in the domain.

Computer Vision: We studied the growth and decline of following topics on the basis of relative number of papers published each topic over a period of years: *human pose detection, image segmentation* and *3d reconstruction*. Papers are included from CVPR, ECCV, ICCV and ICPR conferences from 1990 to 2012. Figure 5 and 7 show an example of trends as extracted from our constructed knowledge graph. Figure 7 shows transition of a topic from aim to method concept in the domain.

Meaningful results in the analysis for both the communities show the scalability and domain independence of our approach.

6 Related Work

There has been growing interest in studying automatic methods of information extraction from scientific articles. Our work maps to mainly two types of problems - Extracting keyphrases, concepts, and relations between them and extracting structured information in the form of knowledge graph from scientific literature.

Keyphrase extraction specifically from scientific articles started with SemEval 2010 Task 5 (Kim et al., 2010) which was focused on automatic keyphrase extraction from scientific articles and prepared a dataset of 284 articles marked with keyphrases. Gollapalli and Caragea (2014) studied the keyphrase extraction problem in an unsupervised setting. They extracted candidates from the title, abstracts and citation contexts and used Page Rank (PAGE, 1998) to give a score to the candidates. Gupta and Manning (2011) first proposed a task that defines scientific terms for 474 abstracts from the ACL anthology (Radev et al., 2013) into three aspects: domain, technique, and focus. They applied template-based bootstrapping on title and abstract of articles to tackle the problem. They used handcrafted dependency based features. Based on this study, (Tsai et al., 2013) improved the performance by introducing hand-designed features to the bootstrapping framework. Our system beats their systems in terms of recall for both aim and method concepts. Also, we worked on larger multi-domain dataset. SemEval 2017 Task 10 (Augenstein et al., 2017) focused on mention level keyphrase identification and their classification into three categories - TASK, PRO-

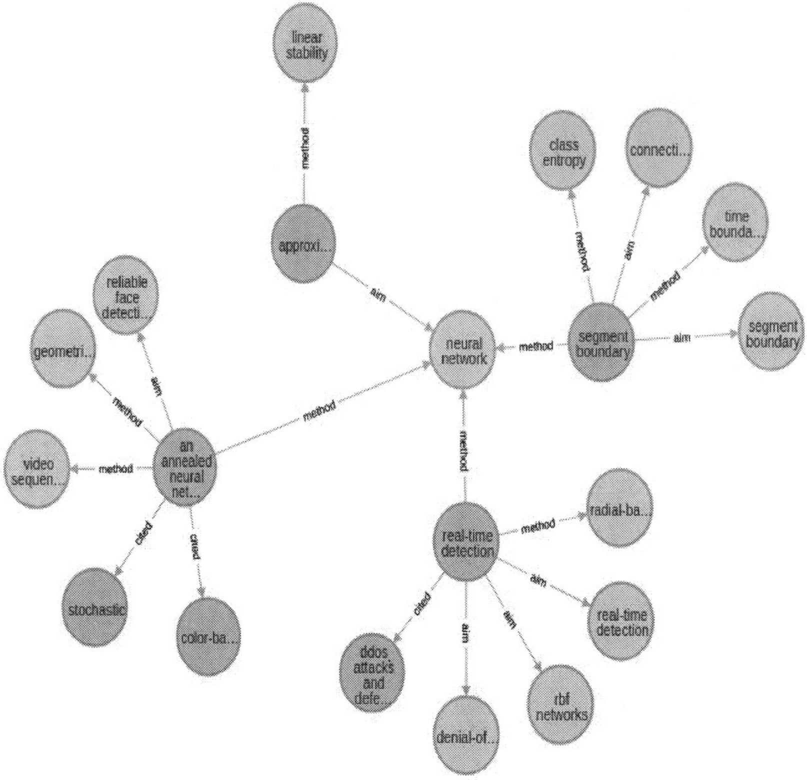

Figure 3: Sample from our constructed graph. Green nodes correspond to research papers and brown nodes correspond to extracted phrase entities.

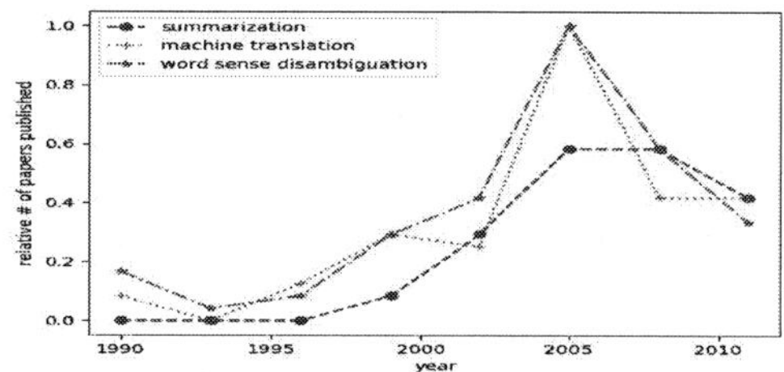

Figure 4: Growth and decline of research in different topics in computational linguistics

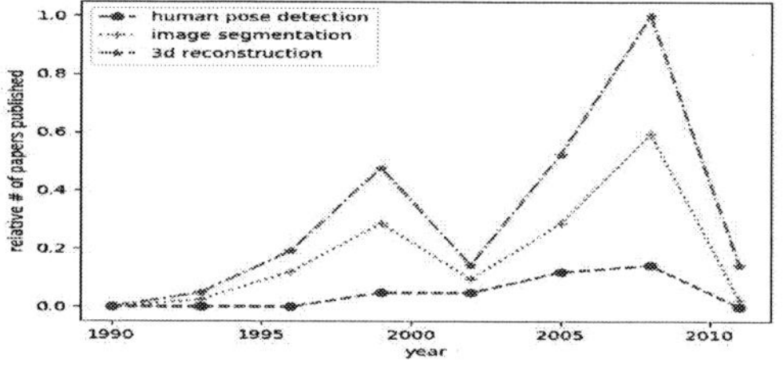

Figure 5: Growth and decline of research in different topics in Computer Vision

CESS, and MATERIAL. They prepared an annotated dataset comprising of 500 papers from Material Science and Computer Science journals. Many systems (Ammar et al., 2017) (Tsujimura et al., 2017) solved the problem in a supervised manner. Top system (Ammar et al., 2017) modeled the problem as a sequence labeling problem. (Tsujimura et al., 2017) trained LSTM-ER on that dataset. However, these supervised systems require a large amount of training data, in the absence of which they tend to overfit. Our semi-supervised method can work using a small set of annotated documents for initial features.

There is also an ongoing work on constructing knowledge graph from the scientific literature. Sinha et al. (2015) builds a heterogeneous graph consisting of six types of entities: field of study, author, institution (the affiliation of the author), paper, venue (journal and conference series) and event. Ammar et al. (2018) focussed on constructing literature graph consisting of papers, authors, entities nodes and various interactions between

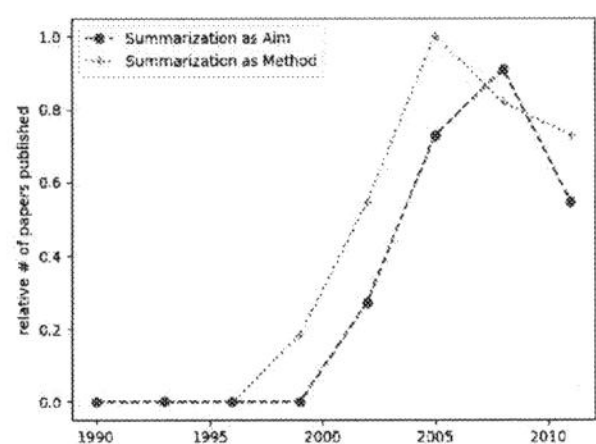 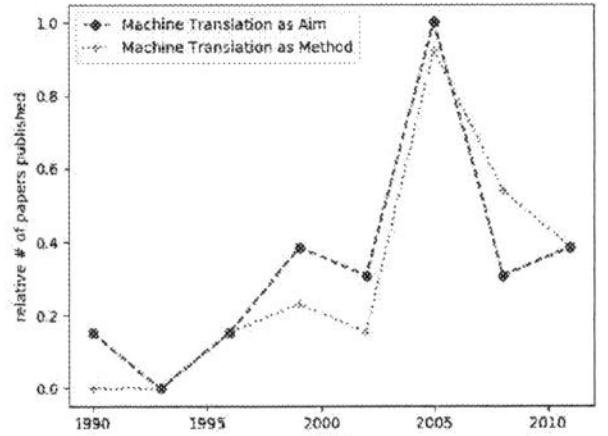 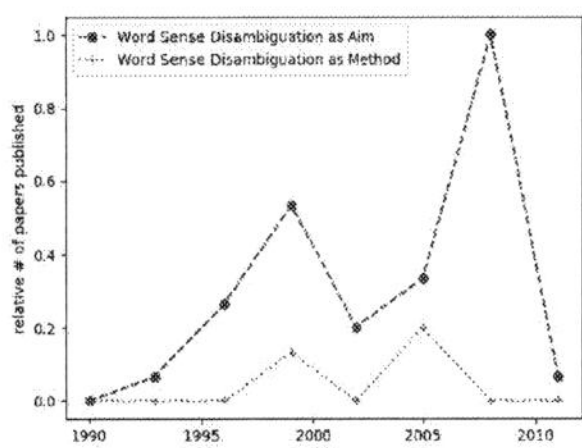

Figure 6: Transition from aim to method for 1. Summarization 2. Machine Translation 3. Word Sense Disambiguation

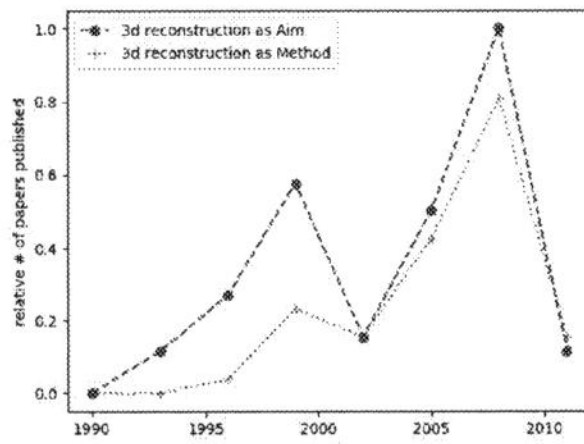 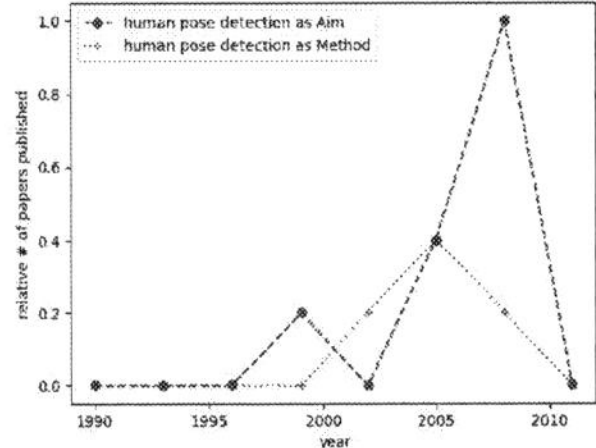 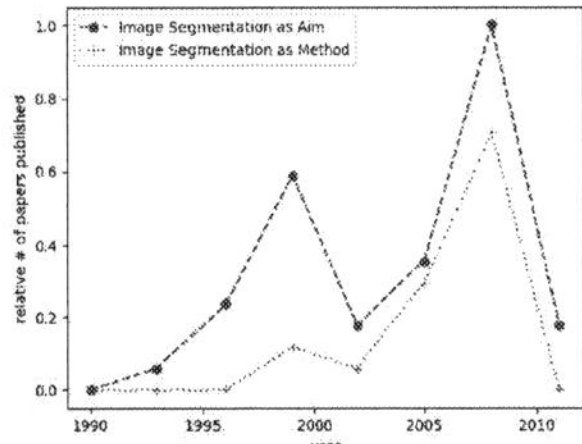

Figure 7: Transition from aim to method for 1. 3d reconstruction 2. Human pose-detection 3. Image Segmentation

them (e.g., authorship, citations, entity mentions). Luan et al. (2018) developed a unified framework for identifying entities, relations, and coreference clusters in scientific articles with shared span representations. They used supervised methods by creating a dataset which included annotations for scientific entities, their relations, and coreference clusters for 500 scientific abstracts from AI conferences proceedings. Our knowledge graph is more straightforward to build. Also, it is built upon the citation graph due to which it retains the vital citation information which is an integral part of the research community.

Conclusion

This work propose semi-supervised techniques for identifying *Aim, Method* and *Result* concepts from scientific articles. We show how these concepts can be introduced in the citation graph to graphically summarize the research community and the various applications of the graphical representation thus formed. We show the domain-independence of our approach as :- a) Seed features from one domain (physics, material science from SemEval dataset) were used to extract concepts for another domain (computer science papers from DBLP dataset), b) Meaningful results for two distinct communities as section 5. We also experimentally show the

scalability of our approach and compared the results with the state-of-the-art.

References

Waleed Ammar, Dirk Groeneveld, Chandra Bhagavatula, Iz Beltagy, Miles Crawford, Doug Downey, Jason Dunkelberger, Ahmed Elgohary, Sergey Feldman, Vu Ha, Rodney Kinney, Sebastian Kohlmeier, Kyle Lo, Tyler Murray, Hsu-Han Ooi, Matthew E. Peters, Joanna Power, Sam Skjonsberg, Lucy Lu Wang, Chris Wilhelm, Zheng Yuan, Madeleine van Zuylen, and Oren Etzioni. 2018. Construction of the literature graph in semantic scholar. *CoRR*, abs/1805.02262.

Waleed Ammar, Matthew Peters, Chandra Bhagavatula, and Russell Power. 2017. The ai2 system at semeval-2017 task 10 (scienceie): semi-supervised end-to-end entity and relation extraction. In *Proceedings of the 11th International Workshop on Semantic Evaluation (SemEval-2017)*, pages 592–596, Vancouver, Canada. Association for Computational Linguistics.

Isabelle Augenstein, Mrinal Das, Sebastian Riedel, Lakshmi Vikraman, and Andrew McCallum. 2017. Semeval 2017 task 10: Scienceie - extracting keyphrases and relations from scientific publications. In *Proceedings of the 11th International Workshop on Semantic Evaluation (SemEval-2017)*, pages 546–555. Association for Computational Linguistics.

Jacob Devlin, Ming-Wei Chang, Kenton Lee, and

Kristina Toutanova. 2018. BERT: pre-training of deep bidirectional transformers for language understanding. *CoRR*, abs/1810.04805.

Martin Ester, Hans-Peter Kriegel, Jörg Sander, and Xiaowei Xu. 1996. A density-based algorithm for discovering clusters a density-based algorithm for discovering clusters in large spatial databases with noise. In *Proceedings of the Second International Conference on Knowledge Discovery and Data Mining*, KDD'96, pages 226–231. AAAI Press.

Soumyajit Ganguly and Vikram Pudi. 2016. Competing algorithm detection from research papers. In *Proceedings of the 3rd IKDD Conference on Data Science, 2016*, CODS '16, pages 23:1–23:2, New York, NY, USA. ACM.

Soumyajit Ganguly and Vikram Pudi. 2017. Paper2vec: Combining graph and text information for scientific paper representation. In *Advances in Information Retrieval*, pages 383–395, Cham. Springer International Publishing.

Sujatha Das Gollapalli and Cornelia Caragea. 2014. Extracting keyphrases from research papers using citation networks. In *Proceedings of the Twenty-Eighth AAAI Conference on Artificial Intelligence*, AAAI'14, pages 1629–1635. AAAI Press.

Sonal Gupta and Christopher Manning. 2011. Analyzing the dynamics of research by extracting key aspects of scientific papers. In *Proceedings of 5th International Joint Conference on Natural Language Processing*, pages 1–9. Asian Federation of Natural Language Processing.

Sonal Gupta and Christopher D. Manning. 2014. Improved pattern learning for bootstrapped entity extraction. In *CoNLL*.

Kokil Jaidka, Muthu Kumar Chandrasekaran, Sajal Rustagi, and Min-Yen Kan. 2018. Insights from cl-scisumm 2016: the faceted scientific document summarization shared task. *International Journal on Digital Libraries*, 19(2):163–171.

Su Nam Kim, Olena Medelyan, Min-Yen Kan, and Timothy Baldwin. 2010. Semeval-2010 task 5: Automatic keyphrase extraction from scientific articles. In *Proceedings of the 5th International Workshop on Semantic Evaluation*, SemEval '10, pages 21–26, Stroudsburg, PA, USA. Association for Computational Linguistics.

Yi Luan, Luheng He, Mari Ostendorf, and Hannaneh Hajishirzi. 2018. Multi-task identification of entities, relations, and coreference for scientific knowledge graph construction. *CoRR*, abs/1808.09602.

L. PAGE. 1998. The pagerank citation ranking : Bringing order to the web. *http://www-db.stanford.edu/backrub/pageranksub.ps*.

Animesh Prasad, Manpreet Kaur, and Min-Yen Kan. 2018. Neural parscit: a deep learning-based reference string parser. *International Journal on Digital Libraries*, 19(4):323–337.

DragomirR. Radev, Pradeep Muthukrishnan, Vahed Qazvinian, and Amjad Abu-Jbara. 2013. The acl anthology network corpus. *Language Resources and Evaluation*, pages 1–26.

Arnab Sinha, Zhihong Shen, Yang Song, Hao Ma, Darrin Eide, Bo-June (Paul) Hsu, and Kuansan Wang. 2015. An overview of microsoft academic service (mas) and applications. In *Proceedings of the 24th International Conference on World Wide Web*, WWW '15 Companion, pages 243–246, New York, NY, USA. ACM.

Chen-Tse Tsai, Gourab Kundu, and Dan Roth. 2013. Concept-based analysis of scientific literature. In *Proceedings of the 22nd ACM international conference on Conference on information & knowledge management*, CIKM '13, pages 1733–1738, New York, NY, USA. ACM.

Tomoki Tsujimura, Makoto Miwa, and Yutaka Sasaki. 2017. Tti-coin at semeval-2017 task 10: Investigating embeddings for end-to-end relation extraction from scientific papers. In *Proceedings of the 11th International Workshop on Semantic Evaluation (SemEval-2017)*, pages 985–989, Vancouver, Canada. Association for Computational Linguistics.

Jim Webber and Ian Robinson. 2018. *A Programmatic Introduction to Neo4J*, 1st edition. Addison-Wesley Professional.

Understanding the Polarity of Events in the Biomedical Literature: Deep Learning vs. Linguistically-informed Methods

Enrique Noriega-Atala, Zhengzhong Liang,
John A. Bachman[†], Clayton T. Morrison, Mihai Surdeanu
University of Arizona, Tucson, Arizona, USA
[†]Harvard Medical School, Boston, Massachusetts, USA
{enoriega,zhengzhongliang,claytonm,msurdeanu}@email.arizona.edu
john_bachman@hms.harvard.edu

Abstract

An important task in the machine reading of biochemical events expressed in biomedical texts is correctly reading the polarity, i.e., attributing whether the biochemical event is a promotion or an inhibition. Here we present a novel dataset for studying polarity attribution accuracy. We use this dataset to train and evaluate several deep learning models for polarity identification, and compare these to a linguistically-informed model. The best performing deep learning architecture achieves 0.968 average F1 performance in a five-fold cross-validation study, a considerable improvement over the linguistically informed model average F1 of 0.862.

1 Introduction

Recent advances in information extraction (IE) have resulted in high-precision, high-throughput systems tailored to the reading of biomedical scientific publications (Valenzuela-Escárcega et al., 2018; Peng et al., 2017; Quirk and Poon, 2016; Kim et al., 2013; Björne and Salakoski, 2013; Hakala et al., 2013; Bui et al., 2013, *inter alia*). This, in turn, has resulted in the use of machine reading systems as the foundation of more complex, higher-level inference applications in specific domains such as cancer research (Valenzuela-Escárcega et al., 2018).

However, the presence of noise in pipelined systems that use IE as an initial component may seriously hinder the quality of downstream results. In particular, biomedical research literature is prone to noise caused by the mischaracterization of the *polarity* (e.g., promotion vs. inhibition) of biochemical interactions. This is the focus of this work.

The identification of polarity in the biomedical domain is complicated by the fact that the language used is often hedged through multiple negations to stay closer to the complex biology underneath. For example, consider the statement: *The inactivation of Bad is sufficient to antagonize p38 MAPK*. Under the (simplified but commonly used) representation of polarized interactions, a naive IE system would extract a negative interaction between the two proteins: `Bad inhibits p38 MAPK`, due to the presence of the negative predicate *antagonize*. However, a more careful reading of this text indicates that the better representation for this extraction is a positive interaction: `Bad promotes p38 MAPK`,[1] due to the interaction of two predicates with negative semantics, *inactivation* and *antagonize*. This situation is exacerbated by the fact that statements in this domain may contain three and even four inter-related predicates that affect polarity (as observed in Section 8).

This paper analyzes the identification of polarity of biomedical interactions, from the perspective of multiple possible methods. In particular, the contributions of this work are:

(1) We introduce a novel dataset that annotates the polarity of biomedical interactions. The dataset comes in multiple variants. A first variant was derived using *distant supervision* (DS) (Mintz et al., 2009) by aligning a knowledge base (KB) of protein interactions (Perfetto et al., 2015) with the outputs of a machine reader (Valenzuela-Escárcega et al., 2018). This dataset contains 52,779 promotion and 35,177 inhibition interactions. To account for the noise introduced through the DS process, we provide a second variant of this dataset consisting of a sample of the full dataset

---

[1]This representation is better but not perfect. The correct representation should be: `(decrease of Bad)` `causes (decrease of p38 MAPK)`. However, the promotes/inhibits representation is widely used both in IE datasets and by a domain expert, so we continue to use it in this work.

that was manually curated by domain experts. We divide this sample into an *Easy* partition where the IE system initially agreed with the KB, and a *Challenge* partition where the IE system's extractions conflicted with the KB. These manually-curated partitions contain 62 and 67 data points, respectively.

(2) We compare several approaches for polarity identification, including a linguistically-informed method (Valenzuela-Escárcega et al., 2018), and several deep learning (DL) approaches. The DL methods incorporate: (a) multiple sequence models that capture the text before/after arguments/predicate, (b) attention models, and (c) explicit features from the linguistically-informed method. Our analysis indicates that: (a) the simpler DL methods perform better than the more complicated ones, (b) all DL approaches outperform the standalone linguistically-informed method, and (c) the difference between the two strategies grows larger with the complexity of the text.

2   Related work

The rate of scientific publishing has grown substantially each year, reaching a level that exceeds the human capacity to read and process. For example, PubMed, a search engine of biomedical publications[2] now indexes over 25 million papers, 17 million of which were published between 1990 and the present. Domain-agnostic approaches, such as open information extraction (OpenIE) (Angeli et al., 2015) can begin to mitigate this by extracting information in the form of relation triples. However the widely varied language used by authors means that extractions can be difficult to aggregate and utilize.

On the other hand, there have been significant efforts to develop domain-specific information extraction approaches that are tailored to scientific publications. These approaches range from rule-based to machine learning-based, and hybrid approaches (Valenzuela-Escárcega et al., 2018; Peng et al., 2017; Quirk and Poon, 2016; Kim et al., 2013; Björne and Salakoski, 2013; Hakala et al., 2013; Bui et al., 2013).

On top of the extractions produced by these methods, causal influence crucially relies on the *polarity* of the influence interactions, i.e., whether

one factor *promotes* or *inhibits* another factor. Biological models have been assembled from these interactions and used for domain-specific applications (Gyori et al., 2017). Here we propose an approach for automatically detecting this polarity.

Polarity detection has been explored in several other natural language processing tasks, perhaps most notably in sentiment analysis (e.g., Pang et al., 2008; Liu, 2012; Liu and Zhang, 2012), where the polarity of a text is measured on a spectrum from negative to positive sentiment. Similarly, in Wilson et al. (2005), the authors frame the problem of extracting opinion polarity explicitly as a sentiment analysis task. Our work is similar in spirit, but it focuses on the polarity of scientific statements. In (Lauscher et al., 2017), the authors investigate the polarity polarity of citations within the context of bibliometric analysis. In contrast, our work addresses the polarity of *content*, i.e., events extracted from the biomedical literature.

To summarize, our approach is inspired by this previous work, but it differs in two ways: first, we focus on statements in the biomedical domain, and, second, we extract polarity for specific, structured events rather than unstructured texts.

3   Linguistically-informed polarity identification approach

In preliminary analyses, we observed that the arguments of biomedical events are generally correctly identified, but the polarity of the interactions is often incorrect due to the complex language used (see, for example, the example in Section 1). Based on this observation, all the methods introduced in this paper assume that an *unlabeled* event is provided, e.g., `Bad interacts_with p38 MAPK`, and the methods then label the event with a polarity type, e.g., `Bad promotes p38 MAPK`.

The first method analyzed, which extends the approach in Valenzuela-Escárcega et al. (2018), relies on linguistic cues. The approach takes the following steps:

1. First, it extracts the syntactic dependency path between the participants in the interaction.

2. Then, the path is expanded to include modifiers of the words along the above path.

3. Finally, the method counts the number of polarity-carrying words and affixes (Bach-

---

[2]http://www.ncbi.nlm.nih.gov/pubmed

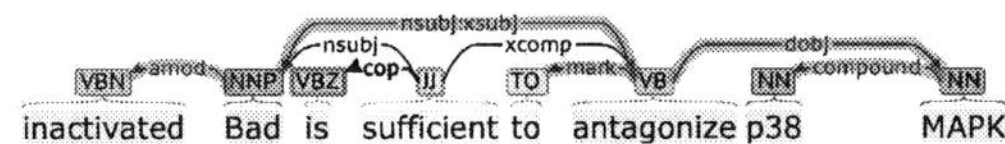

Figure 1: Example of the linguistically-informed approach. From the syntactic dependency tree, the approach extracts the shortest undirected path between the participants in the interaction, *Bad* and *p38 MAPK*: `nsubj:xsubj> dobj>`, where the > and < markers indicate the direction of a dependency arc. Then, the path is extended with modifiers of the elements on the path: `amod< nsubj:xsubj> mark< dobj> compound<`. (The complete path is highlighted and the negative words are underlined.) Lastly, the approach counts the number of polarity-carrying words along this path. An odd number indicates negative event polarity; otherwise the polarity is positive. In this example, the polarity is positive because there is an even number of polarity words: *inactivated* and *antagonize*.

man et al., 2018) from a defined lexicon. This lexicon contains 33 elements, such as "inhibition" and "loss". The event is labeled with negative polarity (inhibits) if the count of these words is odd. Otherwise, the polarity of the event is positive (promotes).

Figure 1 shows a walkthrough of this algorithm for the sentence *Inactivated Bad is sufficient to antagonize p38 MAPK*, which contains an event connecting the two entities *Bad* and *p38 MAPK*. Step 2 of this algorithm is crucial, as many polarity-carrying words, e.g., *inactivated*, do not appear along the syntactic dependency path between the event arguments, but rather modify terms on the path.

We extended the original algorithm in Valenzuela-Escárcega et al. (2018) as follows:

- We made the polarity lexicon case-insensitive.

- We changed the algorithm to match the words in the polarity lexicon only if they occur as a full word or as a prefix, instead of any substring of a word. For example, in the text *Reduction of triglyceride synthesis without affecting **ALLN-inhibitable** protease*, the original algorithm generates a false positive by matching *inhibit* in *ALLN-inhibitable*.

- We handle verb particles, which were ignored in the original algorithm. For example, in the text *The Wip1 gene is overexpressed by switching off p53*, the polarity of the interaction cannot be detected from the predicate alone (*switching*) without its attached particle (*off*).

- We adjusted the polarity lexicon, e.g., we removed *target*; and we added the suffix -*KD* (Bachman et al., 2018), which stands for *knockdown*.

4 Deep learning polarity identification approaches

We propose several deep learning approaches for the classification of event polarity. In general, all proposed approaches use recurrent neural network (RNN) architectures, which incorporate both lexical and structural information into the learning process by considering one or more sequences of words from the source sentence for the given event.

In each of the RNN model variants we investigate, the input sentence is represented as a sequence of word embeddings. Every word w_t triggers a recurrent state that generates a hidden vector h_t, which encodes information about the input word subsequence $1..t$. The output of the RNN is a sequence $\{h_t\}$ of hidden vectors, one for each of the input words.

The hidden vector sequence is then aggregated using one of a couple of different strategies (as described in the next two sub-sections), and then passed forward as the input to a multi-layer perceptron (MLP) that performs binary classification of the event's polarity: positive or negative.

Because our approach applies to biochemical events, we use the result of the underlying IE method to encode the predicate of the event, or its *trigger*, as a feature in the MLP. That is, if the trigger belongs to the lexicon of positive-polarity terms, such as *promotes* or *activates*, the network uses this as evidence for positive polarity. Conversely, if the trigger belongs to the negative-polarity lexicon, such as *inhibits*, the trigger is evidence of negative polarity. We use the same dictionary of polarity-carrying words as the linguistically-informed method.

We investigated two families of architectures: (a) passing the entire input sentence to a single recurrent network, and (b) splitting the sentence into several semantic segments and passing these fragments to independent RNNs (see Figure 2).

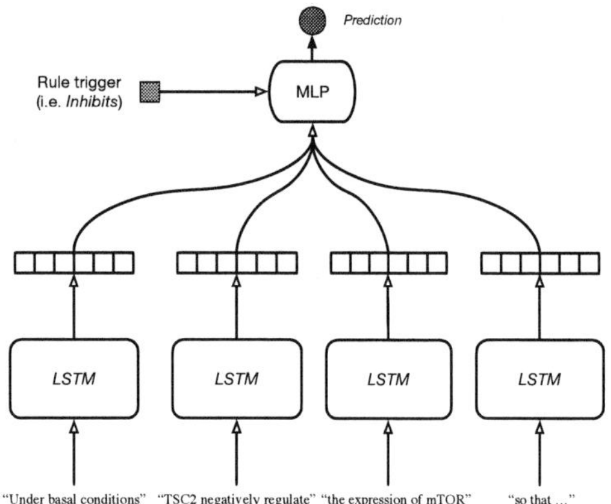

Figure 2: Four-segment LSTM architecture for polarity identification. The four segments model: the text before the left-most event argument, the text between the left-most argument and the event predicate, the text between the predicate and the right-most argument; and the text after the right-most argument. The outputs of the four LSTMs are integrated through a MLP, which also uses the polarity of the event trigger as an explicit feature.

We describe these approaches in the next two subsections.

4.1 Single-segment architecture

For this variant of the architecture, we consider the input sequence, consisting of the span of text that belongs to the event as a single unit, and take the last vector of the hidden sequence as input to the MLP, discarding the rest of the sequence's hidden states. The output of the MLP directly labels the polarity of the event on top of this hidden state vector.

4.2 Four-segment architecture

The structure of the biochemical events modeled here have the following elements: *controller* (or cause), *trigger* (or predicate), and *controlled* (or theme). These elements are text-bounded and partition the source sentence into *four* regions: a window of text *before* the controller, up to three words, the text *between* the controller and the trigger, the text *between* the trigger and the controlled and the window of text *after* the controlled. If the trigger appears before or after both, controller and controlled (i.e. *the phosphorylation of ERK by MEK*), then the event text is considered as a single segment instead of two.

Each of the four sections of the source sentence is then fed to an independent LSTM using the same strategy as in Section 4.1. Figure 2 illustrates

how the sentence *Under basal conditions, TSC2 negatively regulates the expression of mTOR, so that ...* is split and processed by this approach. The last vectors of the four hidden sequences are concatenated and passed as input to MLP for polarity classification.

4.3 Additional enhancements

We implemented and tested the following enhancements with both the single-segment and four-segment architectures from Sections 4.1 and 4.2 respectively.

Pre-trained word embeddings

We used Word2Vec (Mikolov et al., 2013) to pre-initialize the word embeddings. We pre-trained these embeddings over the open-access subset of PubMed Central[3]. We used dimension 100 for these vectors.

Character-level embeddings

To capture information present in the morphological structure of a word, we extended our approaches to use *character-level embeddings*. Each word w in an input sentence is enhanced by adding character-level embeddings to its word embedding e^w.

Given the characters of word w, each is mapped to an embedding e^c. The resulting sequence of character embeddings $\{e^c_t\}$ is then passed forwards and backwards through a *bi-directional GRU* (Goldberg, 2017). Then, the last hidden vectors of the forward and backward GRUs are concatenated into the word's characters embedding e^{wc}.

The word embedding and the word's characters embedding are then concatenated into an enhanced word embedding $e^{w'} = [e^w; e^{wc}]$, which is passed as input for the current word of our polarity network architecture.

Attention mechanisms for aggregation

So far, in all proposed approaches the last element of a sequence has been used as input to the MLP for classification. By doing this, the remaining sequence leading to the selected hidden vector is discarded with respect to classification. To account for this potential limitation, we implemented attention mechanisms (Bahdanau et al., 2014) to ag-

____
[3]https://www.ncbi.nlm.nih.gov/pmc/tools/openftlist/

24

gregate all the hidden vectors into the classification step of the network.

The attention mechanism functions as a weighted average of a sequence $\{h_t\}$ of vectors dictated by $\sum_t^T \alpha_t h_t$. The weight parameters $\{\alpha_t\}$ are learnt jointly with the rest of the network parameters. The scalar coefficient α_t for the vector h_t is computed using the linear combination: $a_t = W_a h_t + b_a$, where the parameters W_a and b_a are shared for all the observations passed through the network. The resulting sequence of coefficients $\{a_t\}$ is normalized with the *softmax* function by $\alpha_t = softmax(\{a_t\})$ to enforce that the weights sum up to 1.

The single-segment architecture is enhanced with this mechanism on top of the sequence of hidden vectors produced by the recurrent network. For the four-segment architecture, we tested an attention mechanism for the hidden vector sequences of each segment of the sentence (*shallow attention*) and an additional approach that also includes an attention mechanism to aggregate, instead of concatenate the four resulting sequence vectors before the MLP step (*deep attention*). This deep attention approach computes a weighted average of the four sequences $\{s_i\}$, dictated by $\sum_i^4 \beta_i s_i$. Similarly to the weights of the hidden vectors, each individual weight in $\{\beta_i\}$ is computed by the linear combination $b_t = W_b h_i + b_0$, where the parameters W_b and b_0 are shared and later normalized by $\beta_i = softmax(\{b_i\})$.

Bidirectional LSTMs

At any given index t of a source sentence, the LSTM network considers only the sequence $1..t$ of words to compute the hidden state vector of w_t. Clearly, this formulation discards information from words to the right of t. To address this limitation, we modified our architecture to use a bidirectional LSTM (Graves et al., 2013) as a drop-in replacement of the vanilla LSTM wherever it is used. Similarly to the bidirectional GRU, the bidirectional LSTM contains two distinct LSTM networks that process the input sentence left-to-right (forward) and right-to-left (backward). The last hidden vectors of both are concatenated and used for the next step in our architectures.

5 Dataset

To analyze the performance of the above approaches, we assembled a dataset of sentences associated with protein-protein interaction events,
as well as polarity labels. The dataset was constructed through distant supervision (Mintz et al., 2009), by aligning events extracted from biomedical literature by Reach, a biomedical IE system (Valenzuela-Escárcega et al., 2018), with polarity labels from the SIGNOR database (Perfetto et al., 2015).

SIGNOR contains approximately 20,000 manually curated protein interactions, the majority of which are annotated with the polarity of the effect of the interaction on the downstream protein (activation or inhibition). These signed interactions were used to establish the true polarities for each pair of proteins in the database. A potential issue with this approach is that an interaction among proteins may have more than one possible polarity depending on the biological context: for example, protein A may activate protein B in cell type X, but inhibit protein B in cell type Y. To mitigate this, we filtered the relations in SIGNOR for those annotated with only a single, unambiguous polarity, under the assumption that for the relatively well-characterized interactions prioritized for curation in a pathway database, the assignment of a single polarity would be a good indicator of "ground truth" for the majority of texts. Processing the SIGNOR database in this way yielded 17,163 protein-protein interactions among with a single polarity, composed of the following interaction types: 13,302 interactions with positive polarity, and 3,861 interactions with negative polarity.

We extracted protein-protein-interaction events from text by running the Reach IE system over all full-text articles in PubMed Central[4], the PubMed Central Author's Manuscript collection[5], and MEDLINE[6] abstracts (for articles not included in the full-text datasets). We kept all information about the events (e.g., triggers, participants, overall interaction type), but discarded polarity information. We assigned polarity labels by aligning these events with SIGNOR interactions that involved the same two proteins and the same overall interaction type, irrespective of sign (e.g., regulation of activity or regulation of phosphorylation). From this dataset we removed: (a) duplicate sentences, and (b) sentences containing events where at least one of the participating pro-

---

[4] https://www.ncbi.nlm.nih.gov/pmc/tools/openftlist/

[5] https://www.ncbi.nlm.nih.gov/pmc/about/mscollection/

[6] https://www.nlm.nih.gov/bsd/medline.html

tein names could not be grounded to an entry in the UniProt protein database[7]. This process produced 68,935 polarity-labeled events (with supporting sentences). For 54,105 of these events, the original polarity detector in Reach agreed with the SIGNOR polarity label (a strong indication that these sentences are easier to classify). For 14,830 events, Reach's polarity disagreed with SIGNOR (an indication that these sentences are more challenging). We call this dataset the *DS dataset* (from distant supervision). Table 1 lists the distribution of labels for the DS dataset on both the Easy and Challenge partitions and overall.

	Positive polarity	*Negative polarity*
Easy	40, 339	13, 766
Challenge	7, 262	7, 568
Total	47, 601	21, 334

Table 1: Label distribution on the *DS* dataset.

The distant supervision process is potentially noisy (Yao et al., 2011). To control for this noise, we also created two smaller hand-curated datasets, as follows:

1. We randomly sampled 100 sentences from the sentences where Reach agreed with SIGNOR, and 100 from the sentences where Reach disagreed with SIGNOR. Based on the intuition mentioned in the previous paragraph, we call these partitions *Easy* and *Challenge*.

2. Because the focus of this work is on polarity identification *given* a correct event, we eliminated the false positive events from both partitions, i.e., events extracted by Reach that were not supported by the corresponding underlying sentence. Further, we removed sentences containing events where at least one of the participating protein names could not be grounded to UniProt. This reduced the size of the dataset to 62 Easy and 67 Challenge examples.

3. The remaining sentences were manually curated by a domain expert. The expert corrected 2 polarity labels in the Easy partition, and 53 labels in the Challenge partition, con-

---

[7]https://www.uniprot.org

firming our expectation that the latter partition is harder than the former.

To facilitate reproducibility, we will release all these datasets (and the software) upon acceptance.

6 Results

We performed a five-fold cross validation experiment on the DS dataset introduced in Section 5 to assess the performance of the linguistically-informed baseline (Section 3) and of the various neural models previously described in Section 4. Note that this dataset contains all the elements from both Easy and Challenge partitions. The data was split randomly and the experiment was repeated with five different random seeds and the numbers reported are the corresponding averages from all the trials. Table 2 reports these average scores as well as the standard deviations for all the approaches analyzed.

Tables 3 and 4 contain the results on the manually-curated Easy and Challenge partitions, when the corresponding models were trained on the entire DS dataset.

The code and data used to generate these results are available at this URL: https://github.com/clulab/releases/tree/master/naacl-essp2019-polarity.

7 Discussion

7.1 Discussion of the main results

Table 2 shows that the linguistically-informed approach performs reasonably well overall, with a F1 score of 0.862. This is encouraging, but also somewhat misleading. The DS dataset consists of mostly Easy examples, where Reach agreed with SIGNOR labels. As discussed in Section 5, the distribution of the examples in the DS dataset is 78.4/21.6% Easy/Challenge. Tables 3 and 4 show that the performance of the linguistically-informed approach, which is an improved version of the method in Reach, drops to 0.143 F1 when evaluated solely on challenging sentences.

On the other hand, the results summarized in Tables 2 through 4 demonstrate that overall, deep learning architectures that incorporate bidirectional recurrence with character-level embeddings perform the best. The reasonable explanation for this is that those specific enhancements are aimed at capturing more global information from the sentence, instead of just the information

Architecture variant	F1 (st. dev.)	Precision (st. dev.)	Recall (st. dev.)
Linguistically-informed approach	0.862	0.859	0.865
Single-segment architecture			
– biLSTM, char embed, no pretrained embed, no attention, trigger	**0.968(0.001)**	**0.967(0.001)**	**0.969(0.000)**
– biLSTM, char embed, no pretrained embed, no attention, no trigger	**0.968(0.001)**	**0.967(0.001)**	0.968(0.000)
– LSTM, char embed, no pretrained embed, no attention, trigger	0.966(0.001)	0.964(0.001)	0.967(0.001)
– LSTM, no char embed, no pretrained embed, no attention, trigger	0.961(0.000)	0.959(0.001)	0.963(0.001)
– LSTM, char embed, no pretrained embed, attention, trigger	0.954(0.001)	0.954(0.001)	0.955(0.002)
– LSTM, char embed, pretrained embed, no attention, trigger	0.948(0.001)	0.944(0.002)	0.952(0.001)
– LSTM, no char embed, pretrained embed, no attention, trigger	0.943(0.000)	0.938(0.001)	0.948(0.001)
– biLSTM, char embed, no pretrained embed, no attention, trigger, mask	0.874(0.001)	0.852(0.010)	0.897(0.012)
Four-segment architecture			
– LSTM, char embed, no pretrained embed, no attention, trigger	0.956(0.000)	0.956(0.001)	0.956(0.000)
– LSTM, char embed, no pretrained embed, $attention_{deep}$	0.948(0.000)	0.949(0.001)	0.947(0.001)
– LSTM, char embed, no pretrained embed, $attention_{shallow}$	0.948(0.000)	0.951(0.001)	0.945(0.001)

Table 2: Deep learning scores from a five-fold cross-validation experiment on the larger DS dataset. The "mask" option indicates that event participants have been masked (please see Section 7.3 for details).

Architecture variant	F1 (st. dev.)	Precision (st. dev.)	Recall (st. dev.)
Linguistically-informed approach	**0.989**	**0.979**	**1.0**
Single-segment architecture			
– biLSTM, char embed, no pretrained embed, no attention, no trigger	0.983(0.009)	0.978(0.000)	0.987(0.017)
– biLSTM, char embed, no pretrained embed, no attention, trigger	0.980(0.011)	0.978(0.000)	0.983(0.021)
– LSTM, no char embed, pretrained embed, no attention, trigger	0.974(0.005)	0.987(0.011)	0.961(0.009)
– LSTM, char embed, no pretrained embed, no attention, trigger	0.972(0.006)	0.978(0.000)	0.965(0.011)
– LSTM, no char embed, no pretrained embed, no attention, trigger	0.972(0.006)	0.978(0.000)	0.965(0.011)
– LSTM, char embed, pretrained embed, no attention, trigger	0.971(0.005)	0.987(0.011)	0.957(0.000)
– LSTM, char embed, no pretrained embed, attention, trigger	0.964(0.011)	0.987(0.011)	0.943(0.022)
– biLSTM, char embed, no pretrained embed, no attention, trigger, mask	0.942(0.017)	0.964(0.017)	0.922(0.029)
Four-segment architecture			
– LSTM, char embed, no pretrained embed, no attention, trigger	0.974(0.006)	0.978(0.000)	0.970(0.011)
– LSTM, char embed, no pretrained embed, $attention_{shallow}$	0.960(0.005)	0.973(0.008)	0.948(0.011)
– LSTM, char embed, no pretrained embed, $attention_{deep}$	0.958(0.017)	0.965(0.010)	0.952(0.035)

Table 3: Performance of all approaches on the *Easy* partition. The "mask" option indicates that event participants have been masked (please see Section 7.3 for details).

Architecture variant	F1 (st. dev.)	Precision (st. dev.)	Recall (st. dev.)
Linguistically-informed approach	0.143	0.138	0.148
Single-segment architecture			
– LSTM, char embed, no pretrained embed, no attention, trigger	**0.757(0.022)**	0.659(0.019)	**0.889(0.033)**
– biLSTM, char embed, no pretrained embed, no attention, no trigger	0.752(0.007)	**0.665(0.011)**	0.867(0.018)
– biLSTM, char embed, no pretrained embed, no attention, trigger	0.748(0.031)	0.658(0.032)	0.867(0.030)
– LSTM, no char embed, no pretrained embed, no attention, trigger	0.733(0.008)	0.648(0.008)	0.844(0.015)
– LSTM, char embed, no pretrained embed, attention, trigger	0.703(0.010)	0.628(0.008)	0.800(0.030)
– LSTM, char embed, pretrained embed, no attention, trigger	0.690(0.025)	0.607(0.024)	0.800(0.030)
– LSTM, no char embed, pretrained embed, no attention, trigger	0.686(0.013)	0.610(0.014)	0.785(0.028)
– biLSTM, char embed, no pretrained embed, no attention, trigger, mask	0.576(0.009)	0.472(0.008)	0.741(0.033)
Four-segment architecture			
– LSTM, char embed, no pretrained embed, no attention, trigger	0.698(0.014)	0.638(0.008)	0.770(0.028)
– LSTM, char embed, no pretrained embed, $attention_{deep}$	0.696(0.017)	0.640(0.019)	0.763(0.018)
– LSTM, char embed, no pretrained embed, $attention_{shallow}$	0.690(0.018)	0.640(0.020)	0.748(0.015)

Table 4: Performance of all approaches on the *Challenge* partition. The "mask" option indicates that event participants have been masked (please see Section 7.3 for details).

found around the dependency path representing the event. Taking into account the full, global information in the sentence as a single segment results in a simpler neural network with fewer parameters, which may also explain why the four-segment architecture, which splits the sentence into subsequences according to the components associated with the cause, predicate and theme, and runs each through distinct recurrent components in the architecture does not perform quite as well as the full, single-segment architecture.

Although the deep learning models generally outperform the linguistically-informed model, Tables 3 and 4 uncover an interesting pattern in the

Number of negative words per sentence	Sample size	Best DL approach			Linguistically-informed approach		
		Precision	*Recall*	*F1*	*Precision*	*Recall*	*F1*
0	49,972	0.978	0.980	0.98	0.873	0.937	0.904
1	16,063	0.90	0.902	0.901	0.694	0.38	0.491
2	2,566	0.94	0.896	0.917	0.773	0.691	0.730
3	300	0.884	0.857	0.87	0.675	0.49	0.568
4	30	1.0	0.92	0.958	0.8	0.48	0.6
5	3	1.0	1.0	1.0	0.5	0.5	0.5
6	1	1.0	1.0	1.0	1.0	1.0	1.0

Table 5: Polarity classification results stratified by the number of polarity-carrying words in the corresponding sentence.

Number of negative words per sentence	Sample size	Best DL approach			Linguistically-informed approach		
		Precision	*Recall*	*F1*	*Precision*	*Recall*	*F1*
0	49,972	0.882	0.934	0.907	0.873	0.937	0.904
1	16,063	0.643	0.627	0.761	0.694	0.38	0.491
2	2,566	0.789	0.734	0.761	0.773	0.691	0.730
3	300	0.744	0.689	0.716	0.675	0.49	0.568
4	30	0.941	0.64	0.761	0.8	0.48	0.6
5	3	1.0	1.0	1.0	0.5	0.5	0.5
6	1	1.0	1.0	1.0	1.0	1.0	1.0

Table 6: Polarity classification results stratified by the number of polarity-carrying words in the corresponding sentence with masked participants.

differential performance on the *Easy* and *Challenge* data sets. In particular, on the *Easy* data set, the linguistically informed approach performs exceptionally well, better than the highest performing deep learning model. The good performance of the linguistically-informed model is not surprising here because, as discussed, the instances in the data set were those for which the linguistically-informed agreed with SIGNOR. But it is encouraging that the best deep learning model manages to achieve this performance as well.

On the *Challenge* data set, however, the linguistically-informed model performance dives to an F1 of 0.143. Again, this is not a surprise given that these data were ones that specifically disagreed with a version of the linguistic model. However, the performance of the best deep learning model degrades just to 0.757 F1, demonstrating the capacity of the model to maintain relatively good performance in the face of more challenging data. We find this very encouraging, especially considering that the neural models were trained on the DS dataset, which contains distant-supervision noise. These results demonstrate that the neural models are able to generalize despite the presence of noise.

Somewhat surprisingly, no attention-based model outperformed the simpler bidirectional LSTM without attention. This highlights that the simpler LSTM method is sufficient to model polarity in this context, and that, possibly, the attention mechanisms are more likely to overfit on the distant-supervision noise present in this training data.

7.2 Analysis of complexity by negative terms

To better understand why the *Challenge* data set was more difficult, we compared the performance of the linguistically-informed approach to the best deep learning model in detail. In this experiment, we partitioned the data from the DS dataset into subsets according to how many negative polarity words (from the negative polarity lexicon described in Section 3) appeared in a sentence and evaluated each subset individually. Training for the DL approach was performed using five-fold cross-validation and the testing scores were computed only for the instances with a specific number of negative polarity words. Table 5 summarizes these results. Unsurprisingly, the scores are negatively correlated with the number of negative words in the sentence for both approaches. However, the linguistic approach suffers a much faster drop in performance as the complexity of the sentence increases. The best deep learning model, however, still attains good performance even when there are more than two negative words in the sentence. For example, the linguistically-informed method drops in performance from 0.904 F1 in sentences with zero negative words to just 0.6 F1 in sentences with four negative words, whereas the best neural model drops from 0.98 to 0.958 F1 in the same subsets. This is further proof that the neural methods are able to aggregate multiple negative-polarity hints from the larger context surrounding the events.

7.3 Masking participants

To mitigate the potential of our method to overfit to the entities present in the events analyzed, we implemented a variant of the previous analysis in which we replaced the words that belonged to a participant in a regulation event, both controller and controlled, with a predefined token that masks its identity but preserves its role in the event. For example, in the sentence *PTEN Plays a Role in the Activation of the PI3K Signaling Pathway*, the participants *PTEN* and *PI3K* will be replaced by the terms *CONTROLLER* and *CONTROLLED*, respectively.

Table 6 presents the results of this analysis. The table indicates that the performance of deep learning models decreases in general. However, the same pattern observed when not masking the participants arises. That is, the deep learning approach is not affected as much when the number of negative terms increases compared to the linguistic approach. Please note that this evaluation is more stringent and could be considered a lower-bound to what can be expected from a real world scenario. It also proves that the deep learning models do capture most their signal from the structure of the sentence in which the event is extracted, and have a degree of resilience when facing participants that were not observed during training. Tables 2–4 also show results for a model trained with masked participants in the corresponding scenario.

8 Conclusions

We have introduced a corpus for the development and assessment of approaches to assigning correct polarity to biochemical events. Using this corpus, we trained and evaluated a variety of deep learning architectures and compared them to a linguistically-informed model.

The best-performing deep learning architectures incorporate character embeddings with a bidirectional LSTM across the entire input sentence, achieving an average F1 of 0.972 in a five-fold cross-validation study. This model was found to do just as well as the linguistically-informed model on examples that the linguistically-informed model does well on, but maintains much more robust performance in the face of more difficult cases.

We also explored a deep learning architecture that splits the input sentence into components that are generally meaningful for the task, but found that this did not reach the accuracy of the single-segment input model, suggesting that there is important information spread across sentence components that should be jointly processed.

Additional work remains. Further work should be devoted to gain further F1 improvement, and the place to start is deeper analyses of the kinds of errors made by the best performing model. Another issue is speed efficiency: the linguistically-informed model processes a sentence much faster than the deep learning models, so is better-adapted for high-throughput use cases. An area of further exploration is to consider the pattern observed in Table 5 and assess the tradeoffs of using the fast linguistically-informed model for simpler sentences (with no negative words) and then use the slower deep learning model for more complex sentences.

9 Acknowledgments

This work was supported by the Defense Advanced Research Projects Agency (DARPA) under the Automated Scientific Discovery Framework (ASDF) program, grant W911NF018-1-0124. Mihai Surdeanu declares a financial interest in lum.ai. This interest has been properly disclosed to the University of Arizona Institutional Review Committee and is managed in accordance with its conflict of interest policies.

References

Gabor Angeli, Melvin Jose Johnson Premkumar, and Christopher D Manning. 2015. Leveraging linguistic structure for open domain information extraction. In *Proceedings of the 53rd Annual Meeting of the Association for Computational Linguistics and the 7th International Joint Conference on Natural Language Processing (Volume 1: Long Papers)*, volume 1, pages 344–354.

John A. Bachman, Benjamin M. Gyori, and Peter K. Sorger. 2018. Famplex: a resource for entity recognition and relationship resolution of human protein families and complexes in biomedical text mining. *BMC Bioinformatics*, 19(1):248.

Dzmitry Bahdanau, Kyunghyun Cho, and Yoshua Bengio. 2014. Neural machine translation by jointly learning to align and translate. *arXiv preprint arXiv:1409.0473*.

Jari Björne and Tapio Salakoski. 2013. Tees 2.1: Automated annotation scheme learning in the bionlp 2013 shared task. In *Proceedings of the BioNLP shared task 2013 workshop*, pages 16–25.

Quoc-Chinh Bui, David Campos, Erik van Mulligen, and Jan Kors. 2013. A fast rule-based approach for biomedical event extraction. In *proceedings of the BioNLP shared task 2013 workshop*, pages 104–108.

Yoav Goldberg. 2017. Neural network methods for natural language processing. *Synthesis Lectures on Human Language Technologies*, 10(1):1–309.

Alex Graves, Navdeep Jaitly, and Abdel-rahman Mohamed. 2013. Hybrid speech recognition with deep bidirectional lstm. In *2013 IEEE workshop on automatic speech recognition and understanding*, pages 273–278. IEEE.

Benjamin M. Gyori, John A. Bachman, Kartik Subramanian, Jeremy L. Muhlich, Lucian Galescu, and Peter K. Sorger. 2017. From word models to executable models of signaling networks using automated assembly. *Molecular Systems Biology*, 13(11):954.

Kai Hakala, Sofie Van Landeghem, Tapio Salakoski, Yves Van de Peer, and Filip Ginter. 2013. Evex in st'13: Application of a large-scale text mining resource to event extraction and network construction. In *Proceedings of the BioNLP Shared Task 2013 Workshop*, pages 26–34.

Jin-Dong Kim, Yue Wang, and Yamamoto Yasunori. 2013. The genia event extraction shared task, 2013 edition-overview. In *Proceedings of the BioNLP Shared Task 2013 Workshop*, pages 8–15.

Anne Lauscher, Goran Glavaš, Simone Paolo Ponzetto, and Kai Eckert. 2017. Investigating convolutional networks and domain-specific embeddings for semantic classification of citations. In *Proceedings of the 6th International Workshop on Mining Scientific Publications*, pages 24–28. ACM.

Bing Liu. 2012. Sentiment analysis and opinion mining. *Synthesis lectures on human language technologies*, 5(1):1–167.

Bing Liu and Lei Zhang. 2012. A survey of opinion mining and sentiment analysis. In *Mining text data*, pages 415–463. Springer.

Tomas Mikolov, Kai Chen, Greg Corrado, and Jeffrey Dean. 2013. Efficient estimation of word representations in vector space. *CoRR*, abs/1301.3781.

Mike Mintz, Steven Bills, Rion Snow, and Dan Jurafsky. 2009. Distant supervision for relation extraction without labeled data. In *Proceedings of the Joint Conference of the 47th Annual Meeting of the ACL and the 4th International Joint Conference on Natural Language Processing of the AFNLP: Volume 2-Volume 2*, pages 1003–1011. Association for Computational Linguistics.

Bo Pang, Lillian Lee, et al. 2008. Opinion mining and sentiment analysis. *Foundations and Trends® in Information Retrieval*, 2(1–2):1–135.

Nanyun Peng, Hoifung Poon, Chris Quirk, Kristina Toutanova, and Scott Yih. 2017. Cross-sentence n-ary relation extraction with graph lstms.

Livia Perfetto, Leonardo Briganti, Alberto Calderone, Andrea Cerquone Perpetuini, Marta Iannuccelli, Francesca Langone, Luana Licata, Milica Marinkovic, Anna Mattioni, Theodora Pavlidou, et al. 2015. Signor: a database of causal relationships between biological entities. *Nucleic acids research*, 44(D1):D548–D554.

Chris Quirk and Hoifung Poon. 2016. Distant supervision for relation extraction beyond the sentence boundary.

Marco A. Valenzuela-Escárcega, Özgün Babur, Gus Hahn-Powell, Dane Bell, Thomas Hicks, Enrique Noriega-Atala, Xia Wang, Mihai Surdeanu, Emek Demir, and Clayton T. Morrison. 2018. Large-scale automated machine reading discovers new cancer-driving mechanisms. *Database*, 2018.

Theresa Wilson, Janyce Wiebe, and Paul Hoffmann. 2005. Recognizing contextual polarity in phrase-level sentiment analysis. In *Proceedings of Human Language Technology Conference and Conference on Empirical Methods in Natural Language Processing*.

Limin Yao, Aria Haghighi, Sebastian Riedel, and Andrew McCallum. 2011. Structured relation discovery using generative models. In *Proceedings of the Conference on Empirical Methods in Natural Language Processing*, pages 1456–1466. Association for Computational Linguistics.

Dataset Mention Extraction and Classification

Animesh Prasad[†]   **Chenglei Si**[‡]   **Min-Yen Kan**[†]

[†] School of Computing, National University of Singapore
[‡] River Valley High School, Singapore
[†]{animesh,kanmy}@comp.nus.edu.sg

Abstract

Datasets are integral artifacts of empirical scientific research. However, due to natural language variation, their recognition can be difficult and even when identified, can often be inconsistently referred across and within publications. We report our approach to the *Coleridge Initiative's Rich Context Competition*, which tasks participants with identifying dataset surface forms (dataset mention extraction) and associating the extracted mention to its referred dataset (dataset classification). In this work, we propose various neural baselines and evaluate these model on one-plus and zero-shot classification scenarios. We further explore various joint learning approaches – exploring the synergy between the tasks – and report the issues with such techniques.

1 Introduction

The modern scientific method hinges on replicability and falsifiability. Datasets are an essential aspect of enabling such analysis in much of modern empirical studies. Datasets themselves are varied — in size, complexity, substructure, and scope — and references to them are also varied — in naming convention and subsequent reference or citation, both within and across documents.

Dataset mention extraction and classification has thus become more critical not only to facilitate the identification of proper target datasets for testing hypotheses but also to benchmark incremental research by extension. In this work, we explore various neural approaches to identifying cited surface forms associated with a dataset and interlinking them. We benchmark our approach on the Coleridge Initiative's Rich Text Context Competition (RTCC), released in 2018, which we participated in, whose dataset comprises of social science publications exemplify such confusability problems with multiple surface dataset citations.

2 Related Work

The extraction of important scientific terms within full-text documents has been desiderata of scholarly document analyses extending back decades. In the early 90s, work by Liddy (Liddy, 1991) explored the possibility of promoting key scholarly document metadata into structured abstracts. Generic aspects of scholarly documents have been explored in (Gupta and Manning, 2011) where key aspects of publications namely *focus*, *domain* and *techniques* were identified using linguistic patterns. Domain-specific corpora with complex taxonomies such as the ACL RD-TEC (QasemiZadeh and Schumann, 2016) have also been employed to train systems to identify fine-grained aspects. In the field of nursing and primary care, the key metadata of *Patients*, *Intervention*, *Condition*, and *Outcome* characterize the acronym "PICO", which has also been the target of much work (Zhao et al., 2010; Wallace et al., 2016).

Recently, shared tasks concerning key generic metadata (inclusive of datasets) have been run in the community. The ScienceIE shared task (Augenstein et al., 2017) benchmarked techniques for identifying predefined entities matching *Process*, *Task* and *Materials*; where the definition of *Material* entities overlap with that of datasets. The task asked to extract such entities and identify the relations among them on short excerpts of scientific documents. State-of-the-art deep learning and feature-based sequential labeling models set the standard for approaches on such tasks, using Long Short-Term Memory (LSTM) (Ammar et al., 2017) and Conditional Random Field (CRF) (Prasad and Kan, 2017) models, respectively.

Though related to a general named entity recognition, we see the problem of dataset mention extraction as having particular challenges. In contrast to the related scientific document process-

31

Proceedings of the Workshop on Extracting Structured Knowledge from Scientific Publications, pages 31–36
Minneapolis, USA, June 6, 2019. ©2019 Association for Computational Linguistics

Publication: ....Source: Monitoring the Future: National Survey on Drug Use, 1975-2009....Section 2 provides a brief summary of trends in adolescent drinking and smoking, using data for the US from the annual Monitoring the Future survey.....Trends in Adolescent Drinking and Smoking: Monitoring the Future.....Systematic annual data on the prevalence of underage drinking and smoking in the US are collected and tracked by several organizations. This section relies on data from the Monitoring the Future (MTF)....
Datasets (Present): [... 56: Monitoring the Future: A Continuing Study of the Lifestyles and Values of Youth, 1984; 101: Monitoring the Future: A Continuing Study of the Lifestyles and Values of Youth, 1989;...]
Datasets (Not Present): [... 100: Monitoring the Future: A Continuing Study of American Youth (12th-Grade Survey), 1996; 108: Current Population Survey, May 1973; ...] –

Figure 1: A text fragment from the training data. Highlighted text represent dataset mentions (citations). Note that a particular mention may refer to multiple datasets. In some examples, as highlighted here, there are many different datasets which closely resemble each other in their surface form.

ing tasks of keyphrase extraction (with 10–15 keywords within a document; i.e., (Kim et al., 2010)) or identify such semantic entities within a small excerpt (identifying which 5-10 tokens constitute entities over 30–40 tokens; i.e., (Augenstein et al., 2017)) dataset mentions within full-text documents exhibits a much higher ratio of sparsity. Further, coreference resolution techniques specific to linking the dataset mention to the dataset have yet to be well explored.

3 Background

We first formally define the task following the specification from the RTCC, as consisting of two sub-problems:

•**Dataset Mention Extraction:** Given a publication (d_i), identify fragments of the text that are mentions of a dataset.

•**Dataset Classification:** Classify the detection mention text fragment to a particular dataset in the knowledge base (D_i).

   Corpus. The corpus is compiled by Coleridge Initiative Rich Context Competition[1] (see the example in Fig. 1) and consists of 5K publication sampled from various social studies, averaging 7K tokens in length. About half of the documents (2.5K) are annotated, featuring an average of 2.2 datasets and 7.5 different dataset mentions per document. Note that some documents do not mention datasets at all. Additionally, the RTCC makes a list of known datasets available (sized 10K), which is taken as an input knowledge base for resolution. Many of the 10K datasets do not appear in the corpus. Hence for these datasets, there is no mention–dataset pair. The corpus allows us to explore the dataset classification problem at three levels of complexity, from easiest to

most challenging:

•**One-plus classification:** at least one dataset–mention pair is present in *training* for all the *testing* datasets.

•**Zero-shot classification:** no dataset–mention pairs are known in *training* data for the *testing* dataset, but the dataset is known to the provided knowledge base. The model knows the dataset description and has to do the classification subtask, but not discovery.

•**Zero-shot discovery:** the scenario where even the dataset (and by extension, dataset–mentions pairs) is unknown to the system (not present in the provided knowledge base). This is also the ultimate aim of a discovery system, which simultaneously needs to populate datasets and their mentions from an empty knowledge base. We do not address this scenario directly in this current work but discuss joint models that can potentially cater to this problem.

4 Model

As the RTCC corpus has only been recently released, there are no formally published approaches, nor public results. However, we have identified that the top performing systems in the competition treat the subtasks of mention extraction and dataset classification as two separate tasks. We explore various neural approaches for both the individual tasks and the look more closely the case of joint modeling. Correct extraction dataset mention is the direct prerequisite task of dataset classification. This motivates us to investigate joint model to perform both tasks. We examine two different realizations of such a joint model that supports multi-task learning.

   Baselines. We model mention extraction as a sequence labeling task. This admits a range of neural models as sequence labeling baselines

---

[1] https://coleridgeinitiative.org/richcontextcompetition

for this task. We start with a Bidirectional Long Short-Term Memory (Hochreiter and Schmidhuber, 1997) ('BiLSTM') model that employs pretrained word embeddings. We then incrementally increase the model's power of representation in other baselines. First, we incorporate a Convolutional Neural Network (CNN) over character embeddings ('CNN-BiLSTM'). Second, we add a CRF layer over the BiLSTM outputs ('CNN-BiLSTM-CRF'); and finally incorporate Bahdanau attention (Bahdanau et al., 2014) over the LSTM layer ('CNN-BiLSTM-Attn-CRF').

Our selection of these incremental components is motivated by the aspects of the problem. Applying a CNN over the character embeddings is introduced to tackle domain-specific terminology that may conserve internal character sequences, such as acronyms found in dataset names. Such names are generally out-of-vocabulary (OOV) with respect to generic word embeddings. The application of the CRF is motivated to reduce token-level noise by incorporating global (i.e., within a sentence input) decoding. The attention mechanism is similarly motivated to focus the model on the specific parts of the input sequence, as datasets and their mentions occur within specific contexts and are not uniformly distributed. The attention mechanism used is defined as follows: first, suppose the sequence output of the BiLSTM $H \in \mathbf{R}^{N \times T \times h}$, where N is the batch size, T is the sequence length and h is the hidden dimension of BiLSTM. Then the model performs the following operations:

$$
\begin{aligned}
A &= H^T \\
A &= Softmax(A) \\
S &= A^T \odot H
\end{aligned}
\tag{1}
$$

where $W \in \mathbf{R}^{T \times T}$ is the weight matrix to be trained and $\odot$ represents the Hadamard product. For the third dataset discovery task, we use sentence classification models *i.e.* BiLSTM and CNN (Kim, 2014) as baselines, replacing the standard sigmoid final binary classification with a softmax layer to enable multilabel multiclass classification.

Shared Layer Extraction–Classification ('SL E–C'). The first joint system selects the best system for each of the individual subtasks, then unifies them by providing a common feature extraction base and optimization using joint losses over both subtasks. We start with the best overall baseline for the mention extraction subtask (*cf.*

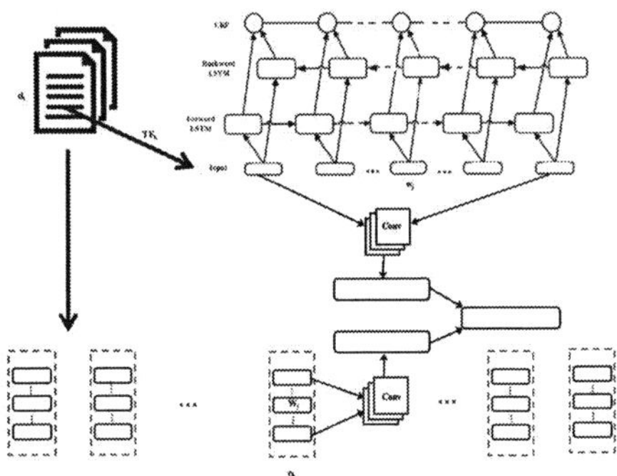

Figure 2: KBSL E–C model. Word embeddings for tokens in each text fragment TF_i (upper left) are translated to its hidden representation via BiLSTM-CNN-Attn-CRF trained with binary labels for mention tokens (upper right). Separately, we apply CNN on the text fragment and all j datasets to obtain datasets representation (individually at a time; bottom row). These are merged and passed to a dense layer, which we train with binary labels to establish which dataset is referenced.

5): CNN-BiLSTM-Attn-CRF. It uses the single CNN-BiLSTM-Attn to encode the textual content, followed by a CRF. For the dataset classification subtask, we share the output from the CNN-BiLSTM-Attn base, and substitute the CRF layer with a CNN layer for dataset classification, as from our empirical tuning, we found the CNN model provides the best performance for dataset classification.

KB Shared Layer Extraction–Classification ('KBSL E–C'). In this model (*cf.* Fig. 2), we leverage on the meta-information of the dataset knowledge base to better support zero-shot learning. There is a description (we experiment two configurations – *name* and *description*) of each dataset in the given knowledge base as part of the corpus. First, we use convolution followed by global max pooling to obtain a representation of each dataset's description text. We then apply convolutions to known mentions of the dataset D_i. Both representations are then merged and passed to a dense layer with a binary output such that $f(TF_k, D_i) = 1$ if TF_k mentions D_i, else 0. This step is repeated for all datasets ($i \in [0, m]$) during testing, and a few randomly, sampled datasets per text fragment during training.

Unlike SL E–C, KBSL E–C can incorporate new classes dynamically by creating a new class representation for predicted new class. Thus KBSL E–C represents an end-to-end zero-shot dataset discovery model.

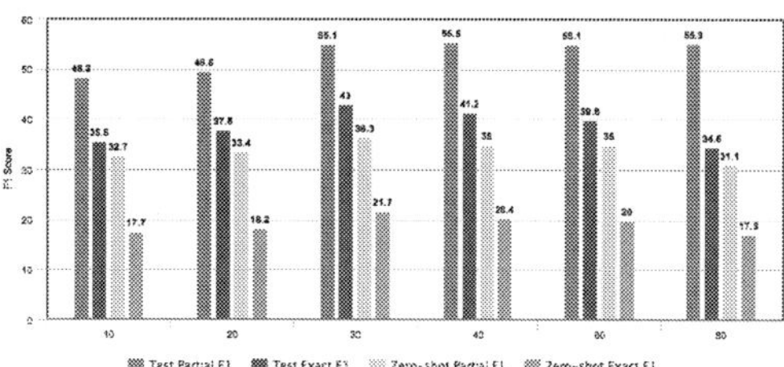

Figure 3: Token ngram-based CRF performance with differing segment lengths.

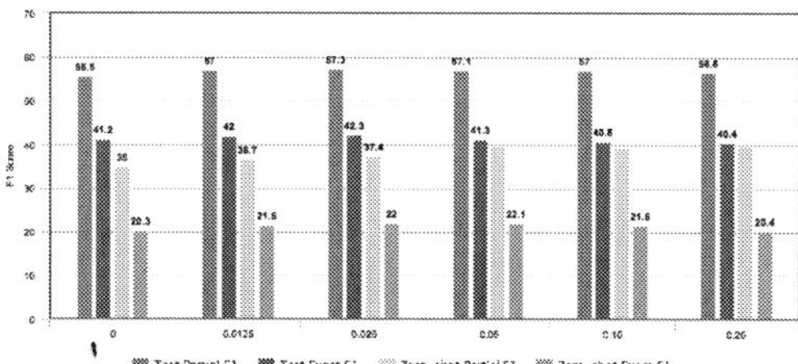

Figure 4: Token ngram-based CRF performance with different NSR, segment length 40.

4.1 Experiment

We elaborate on the complete experimental setup, which has the following configuration:

Hyper-parameters. As the documents in the corpus have 7K tokens on average, the sequence lengths are too long for any model to process directly. We split the documents into shorter text fragment (TF_i) for training and inference. Most fragments do not contain any dataset mentions; these segments we term "negative segments".

The document collection is thus highly skewed, with only 0.4% positive tokens (similarly for positive segments). We under-sample to lessen the effect of data skew, by only considering some of the negative segments during training. We sample all "positive segments", those with dataset mentions.

Our processing methods involve two hyper-parameters – the segment length and the sampling rate of negative segments. Both hyper-parameters affect the ratio of negative tokens sampled in the training set, which in turn impacts performance. We experiment with the CRF baseline model (trigram model, whose hand-tuned features include uppercasing and digits) to analyze the effect of these hyper-parameters and select optimal values (*cf.* Fig. 3 and Fig. 4). For example, a negative sampling rate (NSR) of 0.05 means that we sample 5% of the total number of negative segments from the original dataset for training; conversely, NSR=0 means every training segment contains at least one dataset mention. Note that even for NSR=0, there are still many negative tokens as each segment only contains a few short mention phrases (4.7 tokens per mention on average), with the rest negative.

From the table, we can see that the model generally works better when the negative token rate is small. We use the optimal segment length 40 and NSR=0.015 (1.5%) for all neural models in this paper.

Model Configuration. For all models, we use the 300-dimensional GloVe (Pennington et al., 2014) word embeddings. All models are trained with Adam optimizer.

For dataset mention extraction, the task-specific parameters are as follows. For the base BiLSTM, we use a hidden size of 100 and a dropout rate of 0.2 on word embeddings. We then used a dense layer with sigmoid activation to determine the probability of the input being part of a dataset mention. For the character embedding CNN, we use character embedding dimension 300, 1D convolution 300 filters, window size 6, and a dropout rate of 0.4. For the CNN-BiLSTM-CRF model, we add a CRF layer on top of the BiLSTM instead of a dense layer.

For dataset classification, the task-specific parameters are as follows. For the CNN model, we use 1D convolution with 256 kernels, with window size 6, followed by global max pooling, and a dense layer for the final classification output. For the LSTM based model, we use a BiLSTM with hidden dimension 100 to encode the input sequence and use a dense layer on the final state of the BiLSTM for the final dataset classification. We use a sigmoid for the final non-linear activation function. As explained earlier, the rationale to use sigmoid is to allow the model to associate a single mention to multiple datasets which appear commonly in the dataset (see the example in Fig. 1).

Evaluation Method. We evaluate our model on the **development set**, the **test set** and on the **zero-shot test set**. We first randomly held out 7% of the datasets from the corpus and select the publications (219 documents in total) containing these datasets to form the zero-shot test set. To be clear, the datasets in the zero-shot test set are not seen at all within the training set. We then ran-

| | Development Set | | | | | | Test Set | | | | | | Zero-Shot Test Set | | | | | |
| | Partial | | | Exact | | | Partial | | | Exact | | | Partial | | | Exact | | |
Model	P	R	F_1	P	R	F_1	P	R	F_1	P	R	F_1	P	R	F_1	P	R	F_1
BiLSTM	71.4	64.4	67.7	31.3	34.0	32.6	29.4	32.1	30.7	11.2	12.8	12.0	25.3	20.0	22.4	6.3	6.3	6.3
CNN-BiLSTM	77.5	75.5	**76.5**	41.4	44.6	43.0	49.8	44.7	47.1	28.6	31.2	29.8	38.7	28.6	32.9	18.0	20.8	19.3
CNN-BiLSTM-CRF	79.1	71.1	74.9	42.7	44.6	**43.6**	54.1	44.6	48.9	35.6	33.8	34.7	41.6	27.9	33.4	23.2	22.7	**23.0**
CNN-BiLSTM-Attn-CRF	76.1	73.8	74.9	39.4	47.7	43.2	58.0	50.0	**53.7**	34.8	38.0	**36.4**	42.6	28.9	**34.4**	17.2	17.3	17.3
SL E–C	77.2	72.6	74.8	39.9	41.6	40.7	40.3	43.1	41.7	27.1	28.4	27.7	29.0	28.0	28.5	16.3	16.7	16.5

Table 1: Mention Extraction Subtask performance. Segment length 40, negative sampling rate: 0.015.

| | Development Set | | | Test Set | | | Zero-Shot Test Set | | |
Model	P	R	F_1	P	R	F_1	P	R	F_1
BiLSTM	73.1	71.6	72.3	27.5	47.4	34.8	3.0	5.7	3.9
CNN	81.3	79.5	**80.4**	42.8	46.5	**44.6**	4.9	5.0	**5.0**
SL E–C	70.6	70.0	70.3	31.8	49.3	38.6	3.6	6.3	4.6
KBSL E–C	96.0	85.9	90.7	17.6	27.5	21.5	0.8	1.1	0.9
KBSL E–C descript	97.5	88.1	92.6	12.3	44.6	19.4	0.5	1.9	0.9

Table 2: Dataset Classification Subtask performance. Segment length 40, negative sampling rate 0.015.

domly hold out 225 publications to form the test set. The datasets mentioned in these testing documents may have other mentions in the training set as well. The dev set is split from the training set (5%) and has the same distribution and length as the training set.

Since the test set and zero-shot test set contain complete documents and do not have any sampling, the distribution is different from the sampled training set. During the evaluation, we do not sample. We first split the test documents into text segments of the same length as the training segments and perform inference with our trained model on these segments. We combine the predicted results as the prediction for the entire test document.

We employ **precision (P)**, **recall (R)** and F_1 **score** as our evaluation metrics. For dataset mention subtask, these metrics can be interpreted in a relaxed or strict manner, with respect to true token coverage. The relaxed, **partial** match metric attributes a true positive count if any of the ground truth tokens are correctly predicted by the model as a mention phrase. The strict, **exact** match metric attributes a true positive only when if every token in the mention is predicted correctly. We also report exact match P, R, F_1 at the document level.

5 Results

CNN-LSTM-Attn-CRF and CNN outperform all the other models in the single task setup for mention extraction and dataset discovery, respectively. We note that the performance of sequence labeling models is not very high even though when the task seems trivial. We attribute this to the high number of text fragments with no dataset mention, result-ing in low accuracy. Similar to CRF (*cf.* Fig. 3 and Fig. 4), the precision-recall trade-off for smaller-to-bigger fragments does not allow for optimization by mere tuning of fragment size.

We further find that surprisingly the SL E–C model doesn't increase the performance of either of the tasks. The sequence labeling task is more sensitive to local information. Ideally, the output of mention extraction should be input to classification and hence prime signal for the classification task. But, we find that the classification benefit from more contextual information than just the mention (in fact we find using extracted mentions works even worse) and hence sharing layers causes mix-up of representations of the text input which isn't ideal for either task.

KBSL E–C model retain the trend of the decrease in performance on individual tasks. But surprisingly the model doesn't perform well on the zero-shot test set. On further analysis, we realize this is caused by the nature of dataset with multiple similar datasets making it easier for even simple classification model to achieve a partial score for classification even when the model has not seen an example of the dataset.

6 Conclusion

We explore the problem of identifying the mention of datasets in publications and associate the identified mention to a dataset. In our experiments we find CNN-BiLSTM-CRF and CNN models work best for dataset mention extraction and classification respectively. We identify that while mention extraction is primarily dependent on local signals the dataset classification uses a much wider context than just the mention.

References

Waleed Ammar, Matthew Peters, Chandra Bhagavatula, and Russell Power. 2017. The AI2 system at SemEval-2017 task 10 (scienceie): semi-supervised end-to-end entity and relation extraction. In *Proceedings of the 11th International Workshop on Semantic Evaluation, SemEval 2017, Vancouver, Canada, August 3-4, 2017*, pages 592–596.

Isabelle Augenstein, Mrinal Das, Sebastian Riedel, Lakshmi Vikraman, and Andrew McCallum. 2017. SemEval 2017 task 10: ScienceIE - extracting keyphrases and relations from scientific publications. In *Proceedings of the 11th International Workshop on Semantic Evaluation, SemEval 2017, Vancouver, Canada, August 3-4, 2017*, pages 546–555.

Dzmitry Bahdanau, Kyunghyun Cho, and Yoshua Bengio. 2014. Neural machine translation by jointly learning to align and translate. *arXiv preprint arXiv:1409.0473*.

Sonal Gupta and Christopher Manning. 2011. Analyzing the dynamics of research by extracting key aspects of scientific papers. In *Fifth International Joint Conference on Natural Language Processing, IJCNLP 2011, Chiang Mai, Thailand, November 8-13, 2011*, pages 1–9.

Sepp Hochreiter and Jürgen Schmidhuber. 1997. Long short-term memory. *Neural Computation*, 9(8):1735–1780.

Su Nam Kim, Olena Medelyan, Min-Yen Kan, and Timothy Baldwin. 2010. SemEval-2010 task 5 : Automatic keyphrase extraction from scientific articles. In *Proceedings of the 5th International Workshop on Semantic Evaluation, SemEval 2010, Uppsala University, Uppsala, Sweden, July 15-16, 2010*, pages 21–26.

Yoon Kim. 2014. Convolutional neural networks for sentence classification. In *Proceedings of the 2014 Conference on Empirical Methods in Natural Language Processing, EMNLP 2014, October 25-29, 2014, Doha, Qatar*, pages 1746–1751.

Elizabeth DuRoss Liddy. 1991. The discourse-level structure of empirical abstracts: An exploratory study. *Information Processing & Management*, 27(1):55–81.

Jeffrey Pennington, Richard Socher, and Christopher D. Manning. 2014. Glove: Global vectors for word representation. In *Proceedings of the 2014 Conference on Empirical Methods in Natural Language Processing, EMNLP 2014, October 25-29, 2014, Doha, Qatar*.

Animesh Prasad and Min-Yen Kan. 2017. WING-NUS at SemEval-2017 task 10: Keyphrase identification and classification as joint sequence labeling. In *Proceedings of the 11th International Workshop on Semantic Evaluation, SemEval 2017, Vancouver, Canada, August 3-4, 2017*, pages 973–977.

Behrang QasemiZadeh and Anne-Kathrin Schumann. 2016. The ACL RD-TEC 2.0: A language resource for evaluating term extraction and entity recognition methods. In *Proceedings of the Tenth International Conference on Language Resources and Evaluation LREC 2016, Portorož, Slovenia, May 23-28, 2016*.

Byron C Wallace, Joël Kuiper, Aakash Sharma, Mingxi Zhu, and Iain J Marshall. 2016. Extracting pico sentences from clinical trial reports using supervised distant supervision. *The Journal of Machine Learning Research*, 17(1):4572–4596.

Jin Zhao, Min-Yen Kan, Paula M Procter, Siti Zubaidah, Wai Kin Yip, and Goh Mien Li. 2010. Improving search for evidence-based practice using information extraction. In *AMIA Annual Symposium Proceedings*, volume 2010, page 937. American Medical Informatics Association.

Annotating with Pros and Cons of Technologies in Computer Science Papers

Hono Shirai[1], Naoya Inoue[1,2], Jun Suzuki[1,2], Kentaro Inui[1,2]
[1]Tohoku University, [2]RIKEN AIP
{h.shirai, naoya-i, jun.suzuki, inui}@ecei.tohoku.ac.jp

Abstract

This study explores the task of extracting a technological expression and its pros/cons from computer science papers. We report the ongoing efforts on the annotated corpus of pros/cons and the analysis of the nature of the automatic extraction task. Specifically, we show how to adapt the targeted sentiment analysis task for extracting pros/cons from computer science papers and conduct an annotation study. We construct a strong baseline model and conduct an error analysis to identify the challenges of the automatic extraction task. Experimental results show that pros/cons can be consistently annotated by annotators, and that the task is challenging owing to the requirement of domain-specific knowledge. The annotated dataset is made publicly available for research purposes.

1 Introduction

The number of scientific publications has been rapidly increasing. Johnson et al. (2018) showed that over 3 million research articles are published annually. It is increasingly difficult for researchers to have a bird's-eye view of current research trends with such a large number of publications.

This study explores information extraction from computer science papers. The main focus of computer science publications involves problem solving (e.g., optimization algorithm). One typical form of computer science publications is presenting an issue and then discusses solutions for it. Specifically, the pros and cons of previously proposed technologies are discussed and propose new technology. Example (1) discusses the cons of previous technologies for coreference resolution:[1]

(1) *While successful, these approaches require labeled training data, consisting of mention*

pairs and the correct decisions for them.
(D08-1068)

Therefore, when computer scientists write a paper, it is important to have a bird's-eye view of the pros and cons of previous technologies. As the number of publications rapidly increases, it is desirable to develop an automated tool for mining the pros and cons of technologies.

Previous works have explored automatic extraction of a wide variety of scientific knowledge to assist researchers in collecting relevant publications. This research direction includes domain-independent approaches, such as Citation Network (Kajikawa et al., 2007) and Argumentative Zoning (Teufel et al., 1999), and domain-dependent approaches such as BioNLP (Deléger et al., 2016). These technologies are the foundation of scientific search engines or knowledge discovery tools, such as Semantic Scholar[2] and Dr. Inventor (Ronzano and Saggion, 2015). Nevertheless, less attention has been paid to the mining of the pros and cons of technologies.

This study performs a preliminary investigation on automatically identifying technologies and their pros/cons from computer science papers (henceforth referred to as *pros/cons identification*). We frame pros/cons identification as the well-known NLP task of targeted sentiment analysis (Jiang et al., 2011) and conduct an annotation study. Futhermore, we build a neural baseline model to identify the challenges of pros/cons identification task. The annotation study indicates that the pros/cons identification task can be reasonably framed as the task of targeted sentiment analysis. The experimental results of automatic extraction show that pros/cons identification is difficult mainly owing to the requirement of domain-specific knowledge. The annotated dataset is made

---

[1]Throughout the paper, an appended 8-character identifier indicates the ACL anthology's paper identifier.

[2]https://www.semanticscholar.org

Proceedings of the Workshop on Extracting Structured Knowledge from Scientific Publications, pages 37–42
Minneapolis, USA, June 6, 2019. ©2019 Association for Computational Linguistics

publicly available.[3]

2 Annotation Scheme

We investigate the task of pros/cons identification task by adopting an existing annotation scheme to our task and conducting an annotation study. Specifically, we apply an annotation scheme from the targeted sentiment analysis task (Jiang et al., 2011), which is mainly developed for mining positive/negative opinion about named entities (e.g. person, products) from twitter.

2.1 TERM

We introduce TERM label to annotate with technological terms. We define TERM as a noun phrase that represents a mechanism, a function, or a method to solve the problem. In Example (2), *recursive neural network* and *AdaRNN* are labeled as TERM because these are types of neural network models.

(2) *We employ a novel adaptive multi-compositionality layer in recursive neural network, which is named as AdaRNN (Dong et al., 2014).* (P14-2009)

Note that we also annotate a general noun phrase (e.g. *our method*) with the TERM label and named entities with the TERM label.

2.2 Sentiment

For each phrase labeled as TERM, we additionally annotate it with a Sentiment attribute, which represents how a technology is evaluated. Following the previous work on targeted sentiment analysis (Jiang et al., 2011, etc.), an evaluation is expressed by three types of attributes: Positive, Negative, and Neutral. These labels represent a local polarity within a sentence and are only judged based on the information obtained from a sentence containing TERM. In Example (3), *the whole-sentence-based classifier* that is labeled TERM is assigned Positive attribute, because it is positively evaluated by the expression *"performs the best"*.

(3) *The results indicate that the whole-sentence-based classifier performs the best.* (D09-1019)

Similarly, the negative attribute is assigned to the examples of negative aspects of technologies.

TERM NEGATIVE

Most previous approaches cannot handle collections of this size.

TERM-P

In this work, we present a new method for cross document corefer

TERM POSITIVE — TERM

Our algorithm operates in a streaming setting, in which documents

Figure 1: The brat annotation interface used for conducting our annotation study.

Neutral attribute is given to TERM if only the neutral features and properties of technology are described in the sentence. In Example (2), *recursive neural network* and *AdaRNN* are assigned to Neutral attributes.

3 Annotation Study

In this section, we describe our annotation study used for creating a dataset for the automatic extraction of pros/cons.

3.1 Dataset

We retrieved 92 computational linguistics papers that contained the keyword "*coreference resolution*" in the title or body texts using Google Custom Search in ACL Anthology.[4] Various methods have been proposed for coreference resolution because it has been a subject of research for numerous years. This is suitable for our trial annotation. These papers we considered were published from 1999 to 2017.

In a publication, the pros and cons of the proposed/existing methods are generally discussed in the introduction section. Therefore, we focus on annotating only the introduction section to reduce the cost of annotation.

3.2 Settings

We employed three fluent-English speakers who specialize in NLP. We assigned two annotators per paper to investigate the inter-annotator agreement. Figure 1 illustrates the annotation interface *brat* (Stenetorp et al., 2012), which is used for conducting our annotation.

3.3 Results and Discussion

We measured the inter-annotator agreement after the annotation was completed.

TERM The percentage of the exact match of TERM spans between annotators was 24.0 %. We observed multiple of cases where one annotator labeled a phrase as TERM, but the other annotator

---

did not. Such examples included *joint inference* and *a learned cluster ranker*. We speculate that this is because these noun phrases indirectly indicate whether a phrase is a mechanism, function, or method.

The percentage of *partial* match between annotators was 38.2 %. We observed that the interpretation of span was sometimes different across annotators in certain cases. For example, one annotator included a modifier such as *a simplified semantic role labeling (SRL) framework*, but the other did not (i.e., *semantic role labeling (SRL) framework*).

Sentiment We calculated the inter-annotator agreement of the Sentiment attributes for 390 instances whose TERM span annotation matched exactly matched between annotators. We obtained a Fleiss's Kappa of 0.65, which indicated substantial agreement (Fleiss, 1971).

Even though the inter-annotator agreement was generally high, there are a few disagreements. The primary cause of disagreements is that one annotator assigned the Neutral attribute, and the other assigned the non-Neutral attributes (i.e., Positive or Negative). Among the disagreements, we found numerous cases where domain-specific knowledge was required. In Example (4), one annotator labeled *ranking models* as Positive and the other labeled them as Neutral. To judge the sentiment attributes correctly, one required the domain knowledge of coreference resolution that *directly capturing the competition among potential antecedent candidates* is appropriate.

(4) *In essence, ranking models directly capture during training the competition among potential antecedent candidates, instead of considering them independently.* (D08-1069)

We found a large number of cases where sentences took the form of concession. In Example (5), one annotator labeled *the pairwise approach* as Negative and the other Neutral. We speculate that annotators were confused because *the pairwise approach* is evaluated positively by the phrase *high precision* in the subordinate clause, but negatively by the phrase *neither realistic nor scalable* in the main clause.

(5) *While the pairwise approach has high precision, it is neither realistic nor scalable to explicitly enumerate all pairs of compatible word pairs.* (N10-1061)

	# TERM spans		
# sentences	Positive	Neutral	Negative
2,058	255	1,100	116

Table 1: Statistics of annotated corpus.

4 Experiments

To identify the challenges of the automatic extraction task, we ran a strong baseline model to conduct an error analysis.

4.1 Dataset

To obtain high-recall annotations, we aggregated all annotations from each annotator pair. We solved the conflicts between Sentiment attributes by employing the following rules: (i) if both labels are Positive and Negative, Neutral label is applied, and (ii) if one label being Positive or Negative and the other Neutral, the non-Neutral attribute is applied. Furthermore, we manually cleaned the data by resolving the conflicts between the spans assigned by two annotators (e.g., *a model* v.s. *model*). The statistics of the final corpus are shown in Table 1.

4.2 Model

We formulate the automatic extraction task as a BIO sequence tagging task. Specifically, given a sentence, the model tags each word as one of {O, B-POS, I-POS, B-NEG, I-NEG, B-NEU, I-NEU}, where a combination of BI tags represents a Positive (POS), Negative (NEG), and Neutral (NEU) technical term span.

We use the BiLSTM-CRF model proposed by Lample et al. (2016) which was originally designed for the task of named entity recognition.[5] Regarding word embedding, we use word2vec (Mikolov et al., 2013) embeddings trained on ACL Anthology Corpus (Aizawa et al., 2018) (henceforth, CL), and ELMo (Peters et al., 2018) embeddings trained on 1 Billion Word Benchmark (henceforth, EL).

4.3 Configurations

For the detection, TERM and Sentiment are judged as correct only if they exactly match with gold-standard spans. We report F1 scores as an evaluation measure. We evaluate our models in two configurations.

---

[5]We use the implementation provided at https://github.com/UKPLab/emnlp2017-bilstm-cnn-crf

ID	Sentence	Gold	Prediction
(i)	*Several studies report successful applications of <u>concept maps</u> in this direction...* (I17-1081)	Positive	N/M
(ii)	*Second, <u>they</u> have <u>limitations</u> in their expressiveness.* (D09-1101)	Negative	N/M
(iii)	*While successful, <u>these approaches</u> <u>require labeled training data</u>, consisting of mention pairs and...* (D08-1068)	Negative	Neutral
(iv)	*We compare the prediction accuracy of <u>memory network</u> with an existing state-of-the-art coreference resolution...* (W17-2605)	Neutral	N/M

Table 2: Examples of the model predictions. Underlined words indicate a TERM phrase span. N/M indicates that the model does not label it as TERM.

Setting	Emb.	dev F1	test F1 / Prec. / Rec.
10-FCV	CL	50.70	49.79 / 50.0 / 49.7
	CL+EL	54.23	52.35 / 54.4 / 50.8
NEWYEAR	CL+EL	53.29	42.69 / 51.8 / 36.3

Table 3: Performance of pros/cons identification.

10-FCV We employ 10-fold cross validation in this configuration. When data are split, we ensure that the paper IDs in the training set do not have an overlap with the paper IDs in the test set. For model selection, we reserve 10% of the training dataset as the development set. We report F1 scores averaged across all folds.

NEWYEAR In this configuration, to evaluate the models in real-life situations, we verify whether the models are able to extract the pros and cons of new papers after being trained on older papers. We utilize the papers from 2017 (i.e. the latest papers) and data from other years as the test and training sets, respectively.

4.4 Results and Discussion

The results are shown in Table 3. ELMo embeddings improve the prediction performance on the test and dev sets.[6] This indicates that contextual information is important for pros/cons identification.

The results also highlight the difficulty of our task. We analyzed the results given by the best model (CL+EL model) to investigate how challenging the task is. Model predictions along with their gold labels are shown in Table 2.

First, we observe that when an input does not include a word that directly indicates a method, then we are likely to obtain a false negative error (i.e.,

the recognition of TERM fails). In sentence (i), the model is unable to predict a label for the term *concept maps* because it does not include a word that indicates a TERM. Sentence (ii) is another case in which the model cannot predict whether *they* is TERM. Although *they* refers to a model, our model cannot recognize it because it does not resolve coreference.

We also discovered that it is difficult to predict Sentiment attributes when the phrase implicitly expresses sentiment. In sentence (iii), the gold label for *these approaches* is Negative. However, the model predicts Neutral because *successful* is a positive expression for *these approaches* and *require labeled training data, ...* is negative.

The performance of the models in the NEWYEAR configuration is poorer than that in the 10-FCV configuration. We observed that prediction fails for sentences that contain unknown words. For example, in sentence (iv), *memory network* is not observed in training data.

5 Use Case

To show the use cases of our study, we parsed 60 ACL papers published in 2017 with our best performing model. One use case is to employ our system with a search engine-style interface. We implemented a prototype pros/cons identification system. We consider a situation in which we want to obtain an overview of the evaluation measures of dialogue responses and we already have several keywords such as *ADEM* and *BLEU*. Given a search query *ADEM*, our system lists pros/cons of *ADEM*, as illustrated in Figure 2. Analyzing the results, the cons of *ADEM* are provided such as "*ADEM tends to be too conservative when predicting response scores*". We believe that this search interface will provide useful information for re-

---

[6] The improvement is statistically significant (Wilcoxon's signed-rank test, $p < 0.05$).

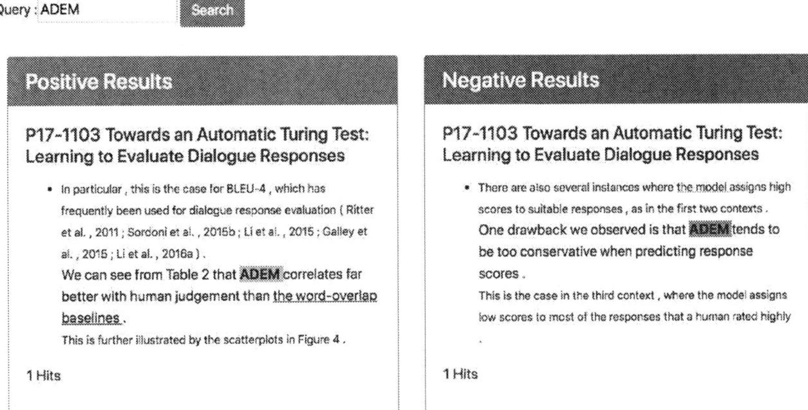

Figure 2: Search results obtained from our pros/cons identification prototype system.

searchers who are starting work in a new field.

Another possible interface is an "add-on" for a PDF viewer. For each important keyword in a PDF, a pop-up window can appear and inform the user about the pros/cons of the keyword.

6 Related Work

There are several types of attempts on extracting useful information from scientific papers. Citation Network (Kajikawa et al., 2007) analyzes the trends of important technology in papers. Argumentative Zoning (Teufel et al., 1999) classifies the sentences in papers into an argumentative type such as BACKGROUND and RELATEDWORK, etc.

A few studies annotate scientific papers with relations between entities such as "APPLY-TO(CRF, POS tagger)". Tateisi et al. (2016) propose an annotation scheme for describing the semantic structures of research articles. SemEval, which is one of the shared tasks workshop in NLP, proposes some information extraction tasks in the scientific paper domain. ScienceIE (Augenstein et al., 2017) is the task of extracting phrases and relationships from papers in multiple domains. SemEval-2018 Task 7 (Gábor et al., 2018) proposes a classification task that classifies the relations between entities in the ACL Anthology. BioNLP (Deléger et al., 2016) aims to extract technical terms, such as proteins, relations between proteins, and substances and their side effects, in the biological and medical domains.

In the field of sentiment analysis, Aspect-Based Sentiment Analysis is performed in the domain of review documents is performed. SemEval-2015 Task 12 (Pontiki et al., 2015) is the task of performing sentiment analysis based on the defined viewpoints such as the prices, cooking or quality of service in hotels and restaurants. Targeted sentiment analysis (Jiang et al., 2011) is the task of classifying a sentiment towards a certain target entity in given sentences. The target entity is the name of persons, companies, and products. In the sentiment analysis in the scientific paper domain, Citation Sentiment Analysis (Yousif et al., 2017) has been performed to analyze the sentiment polarity of an author against documents cited in a paper. However, targeted sentiment analysis of the paper content itself has not been explored.

7 Conclusion

We have proposed the task of pros/cons identification. We have designed a scheme for annotating technological terms and its pros/cons. An annotation study shows that annotators can consistently annotate sentiment attributes. Experiments performed on automatic extraction show that the task is still challenging because domain-specific knowledge and inference are required.

In our future work, we plan to expand our annotation to other domains such as computer vision. We also plan to develop a mechanism of recognizing sentiment attributes using domain-specific knowledge.

Acknowledgments

This work was supported by JST CREST Grant Number JPMJCR1513.

References

Akiko Aizawa, Takeshi Sagara, Kenichi Iwatsuki, and Goran Topic. 2018. Construction of a new acl anthology corpus for deeper analysis of scientific papers. In *Third International Workshop on SCIentific DOCument Analysis (SCIDOCA-2018)*.

Isabelle Augenstein, Mrinal Das, Sebastian Riedel, Lakshmi Vikraman, and Andrew McCallum. 2017. Semeval 2017 task 10: Scienceie - extracting keyphrases and relations from scientific publications. In *Proceedings of the 11th International Workshop on Semantic Evaluation (SemEval-2017)*, pages 546–555, Vancouver, Canada. Association for Computational Linguistics.

Louise Deléger, Robert Bossy, Estelle Chaix, Mouhamadou Ba, Arnaud Ferré, Philippe Bessières, and Claire Nédellec. 2016. Overview of the bacteria biotope task at bionlp shared task 2016. In *Proceedings of the 4th BioNLP Shared Task Workshop*, pages 12–22, Berlin, Germany. Association for Computational Linguistics.

Joseph L Fleiss. 1971. Measuring nominal scale agreement among many raters. *Psychological bulletin*, 76(5):378.

Kata Gábor, Davide Buscaldi, Anne-Kathrin Schumann, Behrang QasemiZadeh, Haifa Zargayouna, and Thierry Charnois. 2018. Semeval-2018 task 7: Semantic relation extraction and classification in scientific papers. In *Proceedings of The 12th International Workshop on Semantic Evaluation*, pages 679–688, New Orleans, Louisiana. Association for Computational Linguistics.

Long Jiang, Mo Yu, Ming Zhou, Xiaohua Liu, and Tiejun Zhao. 2011. Target-dependent twitter sentiment classification. In *Proceedings of the 49th Annual Meeting of the Association for Computational Linguistics: Human Language Technologies*, pages 151–160, Portland, Oregon, USA. Association for Computational Linguistics.

Rob Johnson, Anthony Watkinson, and M Wabe. 2018. The stm report. *An overview of scientific and scholarly publishing. 5th edition October.*

Yuya Kajikawa, Junko Ohno, Yoshiyuki Takeda, Katsumori Matsushima, and Hiroshi Komiyama. 2007. Creating an academic landscape of sustainability science: an analysis of the citation network. *Sustainability Science*, 2(2):221.

Guillaume Lample, Miguel Ballesteros, Sandeep Subramanian, Kazuya Kawakami, and Chris Dyer. 2016. Neural architectures for named entity recognition. In *Proceedings of the 2016 Conference of the North American Chapter of the Association for Computational Linguistics: Human Language Technologies*, pages 260–270. Association for Computational Linguistics.

Tomas Mikolov, Ilya Sutskever, Kai Chen, Greg Corrado, and Jeffrey Dean. 2013. Distributed representations of words and phrases and their compositionality. In *Proceedings of the 26th International Conference on Neural Information Processing Systems - Volume 2*, NIPS'13, pages 3111–3119, USA. Curran Associates Inc.

Matthew Peters, Mark Neumann, Mohit Iyyer, Matt Gardner, Christopher Clark, Kenton Lee, and Luke Zettlemoyer. 2018. Deep contextualized word representations. In *Proceedings of the 2018 Conference of the North American Chapter of the Association for Computational Linguistics: Human Language Technologies*, pages 2227–2237. Association for Computational Linguistics.

Maria Pontiki, Dimitris Galanis, Haris Papageorgiou, Suresh Manandhar, and Ion Androutsopoulos. 2015. Semeval-2015 task 12: Aspect based sentiment analysis. In *Proceedings of the 9th International Workshop on Semantic Evaluation (SemEval 2015)*, pages 486–495, Denver, Colorado. Association for Computational Linguistics.

Francesco Ronzano and Horacio Saggion. 2015. Dr. inventor framework: Extracting structured information from scientific publications. In *International Conference on Discovery Science*, pages 209–220. Springer.

Pontus Stenetorp, Sampo Pyysalo, Goran Topić, Tomoko Ohta, Sophia Ananiadou, and Jun'ichi Tsujii. 2012. brat: a web-based tool for nlp-assisted text annotation. In *Proceedings of Conference of the European Chapter of the Association for Computational Linguistics*, pages 102–107. Association for Computational Linguistics.

Yuka Tateisi, Tomoko Ohta, Sampo Pyysalo, Yusuke Miyao, and Akiko Aizawa. 2016. Typed entity and relation annotation on computer science papers. In *Proceedings of the Tenth International Conference on Language Resources and Evaluation (LREC 2016)*, Paris, France. European Language Resources Association (ELRA).

Simone Teufel et al. 1999. *Argumentative zoning: Information extraction from scientific text*. Ph.D. thesis, Citeseer.

Abdallah Yousif, Zhendong Niu, John K. Tarus, and Arshad Ahmad. 2017. A survey on sentiment analysis of scientific citations. *Artificial Intelligence Review*.

Browsing Health: Information Extraction to Support New Interfaces for Accessing Medical Evidence

Soham Parikh[1], Elizabeth Conrad[2], Oshin Agarwal[1],
Iain J. Marshall[3], Byron C. Wallace[4], Ani Nenkova[1]
[1] University of Pennsylvania, [2] University of Alabama,
[3] King's College London, [4] Northeastern University
{sohamp,oagarwal,nenkova}@seas.upenn.edu
ecconrad1@crimson.ua.edu
iain.marshall@kcl.ac.uk, b.wallace@northeastern.edu

Abstract

Standard paradigms for search do not work well in the medical context. Typical information needs, such as retrieving a full list of medical interventions for a given condition, or finding the reported efficacy of a particular treatment with respect to a specific outcome of interest cannot be straightforwardly posed in typical text-box search. Instead, we propose faceted-search in which a user specifies a condition and then can browse treatments and outcomes that have been evaluated. Choosing from these, they can access randomized control trials (RCTs) describing individual studies. Realizing such a view of the medical evidence requires information extraction techniques to identify the population, interventions, and outcome measures in an RCT. Patients, health practitioners, and biomedical librarians all stand to benefit from such innovation in search of medical evidence. We present an initial prototype of such an interface applied to pre-registered clinical studies. We also discuss pilot studies into the applicability of information extraction methods to allow for similar access to all published trial results.

1 Introduction

The most authoritative evidence regarding the efficacy of medical treatments is contained in papers describing results from randomized control trials (RCTs) (Byar et al., 1976). Evidence-based approaches to deciding standards of care require effective access to this literature, which may entail searching for information that the user does not have at the outset of their search (Relevo, 2012). Medical librarians (Crum and Cooper, 2013), practitioners, and patients would all benefit from a system that makes access to RCTs faster and more intuitive *via browsing capabilities.*

One of the obstacles to accessing RCT papers is that users may not begin with a well-formulated information need. For example a user may want to see what treatments have been studied for a given condition. Perhaps more importantly, individuals will value various health outcomes differently: some will have more interest in studies that used a particular criterion (outcome) to measure treatment effectiveness than in other studies.

For example, someone searching for treatments to control diabetes may be interested in knowing the extent to which treatments might prevent vision problems. But many trials studying diabetes use as the primary outcome measure changes in A1c, i.e. measurements indicative of average blood sugar levels over a couple of months. There is no correlation between A1c and retinopathy at least at diagnosis time (Maa and Sullivan, 2007). Being able to see a list of outcomes and selecting those of highest interest to preform a search for RCTs that talk about vision problems as well would be likely appreciated by users. Using surrogate outcome measures like A1c is considered as one of the core reasons ineffective or even harmful medical practices get adopted as standards of care (Chapter 3, (Prasad and Cifu, 2015)).

Here we present: *(i)* a faceted-search view to browse and search for medical literature based on the condition being studied (and other participant characteristics) in the study, the interventions used, and the outcomes measured; *(ii)* a prototype for the search of clinical studies on clinicaltrials.gov using study metadata; *(iii)* a study to determine the feasibility of using information extraction systems to extend this search to papers.

2 Browsing `ClinicalTrials.gov`

`ClinicalTrials.gov` is a centralized repository of clinical studies conducted around the world. Studies are registered by researchers who populate a number of required fields, such as the

Proceedings of the Workshop on Extracting Structured Knowledge from Scientific Publications, pages 43–47
Minneapolis, USA, June 6, 2019. ©2019 Association for Computational Linguistics

medical condition being studied, demographic information pertaining to the patients to be enrolled in the study (e.g., women, men, children), the medical interventions under consideration (e.g., specific drugs) and the outcomes that will be measured to determine success (or failure) of the medical intervention (such as the retinopathy and A1c example just discussed). The search interface provides a limited faceted-search ability[1] and a preview of interventions. It however does not provide capabilities to preview and select studies by type of intervention/outcome.

We provide a sense of how faceted search interface would work generally for RCT papers by initially providing this view over trials contained within `ClinicalTrials.gov`. The demo can be accessed here: `https://browsing-health.herokuapp.com/`.

Users can see at a glance typical outcome measures used in studies, and they can access studies that considered specific outcomes of interest. For example a search for 'asthma' reveals that the most commonly used outcome is *time to first severe asthma exacerbation*, a direct measure of effectiveness, while the second most used is 'fev1', a measurement of lung function which is a convenient but indirect surrogate measure – lung function can improve without affecting the number of severe exacerbations. Overall, the most common outcome measures across all registered studies were *overall survival, progression free survival, response rate* and *quality of life*.

Patient advocates, medical researchers and policy makers may benefit from this view of interventions and outcomes data, namely by using it to inform care and plan future studies. However, this search prototype was created using the metadata manually provided by researchers at the time of registration. This does not scale to handle the entire corpus of published evidence.

3 IE for RCTs

To organize all medical papers describing RCTs under a similar view, we need automated methods for extracting patient, intervention, and outcome descriptions from the abstracts (or full-texts) of articles describing trials. In this section we use pre-trained models for sequence labeling for these three aspects of RCTs (Nye et al., 2018). These are

standard LSTM-CRF models (Huang et al., 2015; Lample et al., 2016) trained on crowdsourced annotations of ~5000 abstracts of papers from MEDLINE (via PubMed) that describe RCTs with human subjects. We use the publicly released pre-trained models for sequence labeling from `https://ebm-nlp.herokuapp.com/`.

In the prior evaluation of these models, token-level precision and recall for coarse annotation of spans is reasonably good[2]. Spans describing participants are marked well in terms of both precision (75%) and recall (80%). Outcomes have good precision (80%) but lower recall and intervention spans have the lowest accuracy for automatic tagging. Here we explore the feasibility of using automated extraction to provide access to the medical literature via a browsing interface.

3.1 Complete label set

First, we ask whether the automatic span tagging can identify at least one span for each for patient, intervention, and outcome descriptors in (most) papers. This is a minimum requirement for being able to display the article via a faceted view. Note that this concern is independent of whether spans are *accurately* marked; a bare necessity prior to this is that any spans are marked at all.

We sampled thousands of abstracts of medical papers from MEDLINE (Greenhalgh, 1997). We used the associated metadata to identify a subset of abstracts for RCTs with human subjects. We extracted patient, intervention, and outcome spans using the pre-trained models mentioned above. Table 1 shows the percentage of articles for which at least one instance of each information type was labeled. Nearly 80% of articles had all three labels. Further, there were almost no human RCT abstracts that did not have any label (less than 1%). On inspection, we noticed that most of the abstracts without any automatically extracted study descriptors were either not actually descriptions of RCTs, or they were RCTs for diagnostic tests, not treatments for medical conditions.

The contrast with the coverage of extracted snippets in non-RCT human studies is reassuring. Only about 15 percent of such studies had all three study aspects labeled. On inspection, these tended to be RCTs in animals or observational studies.

We tested the coverage of automated extrac-

---

[1]`https://clinicaltrials.gov/ct2/results?cond=diabetes`

[2]See the leaderboard at `http://www.ebm-nlp.com/#Leaderboard`

Type of Article	% with 3 labels	% with no labels
Human RCT	76.72	0.77
Other abstracts	14.42	21.00

Table 1: Percentage of abstracts of papers describing human RCTs (337k) with all three study elements marked and no study element marked. This is contrasted with extracts from other papers (106k), either not RCTs or not with human subjects.

Type of Article	% with 3 labels	% with no labels
Structured	78.45	0.27
Unstructured	74.12	1.50

Table 2: The percentage of structured (176k) and unstructured (161k) abstracts of RCT humans studies for which all three/no descriptors are extracted.

		Unseen		Seen	
	N	Unique	Total	Unique	Total
P	1	13.88%	407k	0.31%	575k
	2	33.10%	822k	3.70%	66k
	3	61.33%	783k	10.50%	12k
	4	80.27%	708k	17.81%	1.8k
I	1	15.22%	432k	0.42%	818k
	2	36.39%	796k	3.40%	107k
	3	64.92%	704k	6.99%	27k
	4	80.55%	595k	12.71%	5k
O	1	9.00%	808k	0.16%	1888k
	2	23.45%	1980k	1.63%	222k
	3	52.72%	1681k	3.72%	61k
	4	73.69%	1387k	6.44%	15k

Table 3: The number of N-grams (N=1,2,3,4) seen during training and marked during inference as well for each label. P stands for Population, I stands for Intervention and O stands for Outcomes

tors on structured and unstructured abstracts, respectively. In unstructured abstracts authors decide what information to include in the abstracts of their paper. Structured abstracts were introduced to ensure that important information is included under an explicit heading, i.e. BACKGROUND, PARTICIPANTS, METHOD, OUTCOME. Different journals require their idiosyncratic structure for abstract but in general these have become the norm in the medical literature. The motivation for requiring structured abstracts is that they are more likely to explicitly and clearly describe important aspect of the described research (Sharma and Harrison, 2006). Here we use this expectation of better coverage on structured abstract as indirect measure of the abilities of automatic sequence tagging.

Here again we use meta-data to consider only human RCTs. Structured abstracts have been found to be more accessible and informative (Huth, 1987), so we expected that an automated extractor would similarly have different coverage of extracted information for the two types of abstracts. As Table 2 shows, this is indeed the case. A larger percentage of structured abstracts have all three study elements marked automatically, with 4% absolute difference in coverage between the two types of abstracts. Even in unstructured abstracts, there is virtually no abstracts from which not a single RCT aspect is extracted.

These results are encouraging. The sequence labeling models behave intuitively and do not mark spans in abstracts where the presence of spans is not expected (as in non-RCT/human study abstracts) or is expected to be harder to find, either because of wording or because it is not included (as in unstructured abstracts).

3.2 Do the models generalize?

Another important question is whether IE models generalize, that is, whether such models mark phrases not seen in the training data (Augenstein et al., 2017). To investigate this, we classify the extracted snippets from MEDLINE data into 'seen' (those that match exactly with or that appear as a substring of an annotated span in the training data) and 'unseen', i.e., snippets that do not appear as a (sub)unit in the training data.

Table 3 provides the number and percentage of extracted spans that do not occur in the training data, broken down by the length of the extracted span. The results are encouraging: even for unigrams, a large fraction of marked snippets are unseen and hence are generalized from the context. As expected, the longer the snippet, the larger the proportion of uniquely marked phrases, as longer phrases are unlikely to be repeated verbatim.

These results suggest that the models generalize well, and can identity novel snippets. This finding is promising in its implications for using IE to power a browseable view of trial data.

3.3 Impressions of Extraction Quality

In this section, we discuss a few qualitative observations related to automated extraction of patient, intervention and outcome information and the implications these have for further computational work on the extraction task.

Figures 1 and 2 show two abstracts with automatic annotations of participants, interventions and outcomes. Overall, the mark-up looks good, with all three RCT aspects covered. For the abstract in Figure 1, the interventions are accurately

This study analyzed the effectiveness of suprascapular nerve block under ultrasonographic guidance in patients with perishoulder pain. Patients with perishoulder pain were enrolled in the study and were randomly divided into 2 groups. In the first group of 25 patients (12 men and 13 women), nerve block was applied under ultrasonographic guidance. Mean patient age in this group was 55.1 years. In the control group, 25 patients (11 men and 14 women) underwent nerve block without ultrasonographic guidance; mean patient age was 51.6 years. Degree of pain was assessed using a visual analog scale (VAS) and shoulder function was evaluated using the Constant shoulder score (CSS) before the nerve block, immediately following the procedure, and 1 month after the procedure. There was no statistically significant difference between the 2 groups in VAS score and CSS before the procedure ($P > .05$). Immediately after the procedure, both the study and control groups revealed significantly improved VAS and CSS patterns ($P < .05$). However , the study group showed better VAS and CSS patterns than the control group at 1-month follow-up ($P < .05$). No complications occurred in the study group. In the control group , there were 2 cases of arterial punctures and 3 cases of direct nerve injury with neurological deficit for 2 months. Ultrasonography-guided suprascapular nerve injection is a safe, accurate, and useful procedure compared to the blind technique.

Figure 1: Example of a Human RCT abstract with the predicted spans for Participants (red), Intervention (blue) and Outcome (orange)

This study aimed at studying the effect of yogic package (YP) with some selected pranayama, cleansing practices and meditation on pain intensity, inflammation, stiffness, pulse rate (PR), blood pressure (BP), lymphocyte count (LC), C-reactive protein (CRP) and serum uric acid (UA) level among subjects of rheumatoid arthritis (RA). Randomized control group design was employed to generate pre and post data on participants and controls. Repealed Measure ANOVAs with Bonferroni adjustment were applied to check significant overall difference among pre and post means of participants and controls by using PASW (SPSS Inc. 18th Version). Observed result favored statistically significant positive effect of YP on selected RA parameters and symptoms under study at $P < 0.05$, 0.01 and 0.001 respectively that showed remarkable improvement in RA severity after 40-day practice of YP. It concluded that YP is a significant means to reduce intensity of RA .

Figure 2: Example of a Human RCT abstract with the predicted spans for Participants (red), Intervention (blue) and Outcome (orange)

identified in the first and last sentence but in addition, a number of mentions of outcomes are erroneously marked as interventions. Importantly, the (same) outcomes are mentioned four times in the abstract. Some mentions are missed by the system, others are mistyped (recognized as interventions) and others are correctly identified. There is a similar problem where the unusual and unseen in training intervention *yogic package* is correctly marked but one of the subsequent mentions towards the end of the abstract is not detected. This observation implies that typical use of precision and recall, either token- or span-level, for evaluation of the sequence labeling may be misleading. Instead, an evaluation would need to capture the degree to which at least one instance of each aspect was captured correctly. Matching variants of the same aspect, such as 'Constant shoulder score' and 'CSS' will also be needed in order to support indexing and search over the extracted elements.

Another possible issue is the need to chunk more complex marked spans, particularly the conjunction of outcomes in Figure 1 and the list of outcomes in Figure 2. Similar need arises in getting the *medical condition* for which treatment is studied, by separating that string from the overall span including 'patients with/subjects with'.

Such granular spans were annotated in the original EBM-NLP corpus (Nye et al., 2018), along with a detailed types of interventions and outcomes. Performance for labeling these details and granular spans however is much lower than that for the original high-level spans that we examine here. An alternative would be to learn chunking rules to identify the condition, individual interventions and individual outcomes in an unsupervised manner, by collocation analysis of the thousands of extracted snippets from the MEDLINE corpus.

In sum, progress on IE to aid browsing of the medical literature would require several modifications to track meaningful progress. Evaluation should be on exact spans that can serve directly as indexing terms for abstracts, and these should measure the ability of the system to find at least one mention of each RCT aspect.

4 Conclusion

We presented a proposal for an alternative mode of access to papers describing randomized control trials. We present a crude example of the browsing capabilities that can be built upon information extraction results from the medical literature. The initial prototype is powered by RCT descriptors written by a person during the registration of the study. We then present some preliminary experiments on applying existing sequence labeling methods for extracting RCT descriptors from the free text of paper abstracts. Results are promising, showing good coverage and reasonable activation of the extraction. We identify aspects in which the information extraction tasks ought to be adjusted in order to better serve indexing needs.

Biomedical librarians are increasingly asked to identify medical evidence in preparation of future randomized control trials and questions regarding patient care. The browsing interface we envision will likely facilitate their work.

References

Isabelle Augenstein, Leon Derczynski, and Kalina Bontcheva. 2017. Generalisation in named entity recognition: A quantitative analysis. *Computer Speech & Language*, 44:61–83.

David P Byar, Richard M Simon, William T Friedewald, James J Schlesselman, David L DeMets, Jonas H Ellenberg, Mitchell H Gail, and James H Ware. 1976. Randomized clinical trials: perspectives on some recent ideas. *New England Journal of Medicine*, 295(2):74–80.

Janet A Crum and I Diane Cooper. 2013. Emerging roles for biomedical librarians: a survey of current practice, challenges, and changes. *Journal of the Medical Library Association: JMLA*, 101(4):278.

Trisha Greenhalgh. 1997. How to read a paper: the medline database. *Bmj*, 315(7101):180–183.

Zhiheng Huang, Wei Xu, and Kai Yu. 2015. Bidirectional lstm-crf models for sequence tagging. *arXiv preprint arXiv:1508.01991*.

Edward J Huth. 1987. Structured abstracts for papers reporting clinical trials. *Annals of Internal Medicine*, 106(4):626–627.

Guillaume Lample, Miguel Ballesteros, Sandeep Subramanian, Kazuya Kawakami, and Chris Dyer. 2016. Neural architectures for named entity recognition. In *NAACL HLT 2016, The 2016 Conference of the North American Chapter of the Association for Computational Linguistics: Human Language Technologies, San Diego California, USA, June 12-17, 2016*, pages 260–270.

April Y Maa and Brian R Sullivan. 2007. Relationship of hemoglobin a1c with the presence and severity of retinopathy upon initial screening of type ii diabetes mellitus. *American journal of ophthalmology*, 144(3):456–457.

Benjamin Nye, Junyi Jessy Li, Roma Patel, Yinfei Yang, Iain James Marshall, Ani Nenkova, and Byron C. Wallace. 2018. A corpus with multi-level annotations of patients, interventions and outcomes to support language processing for medical literature. In *Proceedings of the 56th Annual Meeting of the Association for Computational Linguistics, ACL 2018, Melbourne, Australia, July 15-20, 2018, Volume 1: Long Papers*, pages 197–207.

Vinayak K Prasad and Adam S Cifu. 2015. *Ending medical reversal: improving outcomes, saving lives.* JHU Press.

Rose Relevo. 2012. Effective search strategies for systematic reviews of medical tests. *Journal of general internal medicine*, 27(1):28–32.

Sandeep Sharma and Jayne E Harrison. 2006. Structured abstracts: do they improve the quality of information in abstracts? *American journal of orthodontics and dentofacial orthopedics*, 130(4):523–530.

An Analysis of Deep Contextual Word Embeddings and Neural Architectures for Toponym Mention Detection in Scientific Publications

Matthew Magnusson
Department of Computer Science
University of New Hampshire
mfm2@cs.unh.edu

Laura Dietz
Department of Computer Science
University of New Hampshire
dietz@cs.unh.edu

Abstract

Toponym detection in scientific papers is an open task and a key first step in place entity enrichment of documents. We examine three common neural architectures in NLP: 1) convolutional neural network, 2) multi-layer perceptron (both applied in a sliding window context) and 3) bi-directional LSTM and apply contextual and non-contextual word embedding layers to these models. We find that deep contextual word embeddings improve the performance of the bi-LSTM with CRF neural architecture achieving the best performance when multiple layers of deep contextual embeddings are concatenated. Our best performing model achieves an average F1 of 0.910 when evaluated on overlap macro exceeding previous state-of-the-art models in the toponym detection task.

1 Introduction

The available scientific knowledge is growing every day.[1] Yet, this knowledge is often locked into publications in pdf format, that are not condusive to machine-reading or automated analyses. In this work we take a step towards automated knowledge extraction that is compatible with extraction and visualization frameworks for scientific publications (Ronzano and Saggion, 2016).

Many scientific publications contain geographic references which are commonly confused by extractors with other entities such as people or proteins whose name contains references to places. Extracting such placenames, or toponyms, has several important applications such as the identification of virus outbreak locations (Weissenbacher et al., 2015), treatment adherence (Zhang et al., 2012), and mapping of research findings (Leveling, 2015).

Toponyms are textual spans of text that identify geospatial locations. This can range from the canonical name of populated places, such as "Chengdu" to direct or indirect mentions of geographic entities, including "Cho Oyu" or "5 km south of Mirnyy". The parsing of geographic locations from unstructured text is often addressed with gazeteers. It is generally very difficult to achieve high accuracy due to domain diversity, place name ambiguity, metonymic language and limited contextual cues (Gritta et al., 2018). Furthermore, major challenges to toponym detection in scientific texts come from the fact that names of institutions, viruses and proteins often contain geographic references. Moreover, the extractor needs to handle the overall noisy nature of scientific articles after PDF extraction—with challenges include associating figures and tables as well as handling character encodings.

Task: Toponym detection. Given the text of a scientific publication (as extracted from the PDF), the task is to extract character offset locations of true toponyms. This location is referred to as a toponym mention in the following. A toponym is defined to include proper names and geographic entities but to exclude indirect mentions of places and metonyms. Toponym detection is a first step towards toponym resolution where each toponym mention is to be aligned to a geospatial location.

In this work we focus on toponym detection and evaluate different neural specialization models for word embeddings on this task.[2] This approach has benefitted many natural language processing (NLP) tasks, such as named entity recognition (Collobert et al., 2011). Previous work in toponym detection has mostly focused on non-contextual word embeddings (Magge et al., 2018). Here we study which neural model and which word embed-

---

[1] In 2016, 2.3 million science and engineering publications were produced globally up from 1.2 million in 2003 for a 5.2% compound annual growth rate (NSF, 2018).

[2] Data and code available in appendix: https://cs.unh.edu/~mfm2/index.html

Proceedings of the Workshop on Extracting Structured Knowledge from Scientific Publications, pages 48–56
Minneapolis, USA, June 6, 2019. ©2019 Association for Computational Linguistics

ding types are best suited for the detection of toponyms in scientific publications. We also demonstrate the benefits of neural architectures in comparison to Tagme, a state-of-the-art entity linker, from which we isolate toponym spots based on DBpedia categories.

The contribution of our work lies in answering the following research questions in regards to the task of toponym detection in scientific papers:

RQ1 Independent of the neural model architecture for specialization, which embedding demonstrates better performance: A task-independent deep contextual embeddings or a non-contextual embedding trained on a scientific-domain specific corpus?

RQ2 Given an optimal embedding, which neural specialization architecture is optimal for the task?

RQ3 Given an optimal word embedding and neural architecture, what are the performance impacts of different combinations of the embedding and the classifier?

Our findings show that the best performance on toponym detection is achieved by deep contextual embeddings (even though trained on a non-scientific corpus) when using bidirectional LSTMs with CRFs as the specialization architecture (Peters et al., 2018), while concatenating the layers of the embeddings. However, other deep contextual configurations including weighted average, and single layer selection also yield similar average performance. We also find that handcrafted orthographic features did not impact bi-LSTM model performance, but did positively impact MLP and negatively impacted CNN.

Outline. In Section 2 we discuss related work. Section 3 explains the neural models types included in our analysis and discusses word embedding types. In Section 4, we provide details on the approaches examined in our study. In Section 5 we discuss the data, metrics, and results obtained. We finish with a conclusion about the research questions posed.

2   Related Work

There is significant work in the area of toponym detection (Matsuda et al., 2015; Lieberman et al., 2010) and the closely related fields of named entity recognition (Li et al., 2018) and entity mention detection (Shen et al., 2015) with many different approaches. State-of-the-art named entity detection models have historically employed a combination of hand-crafted features, rules, natural language processing, string-pattern matching, and domain knowledge using supervised learning on relatively-small manually annotated corpora (Piskorski and Yangarber, 2013). A common approach to toponym detection has been to utilize place name gazetteers which are directories of geographic names and their corresponding geolocations to perform string matching of place names in text (Lieberman et al., 2010).

Contemporary approaches in entity detection have included conditional random fields (CRF) (Lafferty et al., 2001) and neural-based architectures. (Collobert et al., 2011) propose a window-based, multi-layer, dense feed-forward neural architecture using word embeddings concatenated with orthographic features and a gazetteer as an input layer with a hard Tanh output layer for superior performance on a standard NER task. Huang et al. (2015) utilise a bi-directional LSTM with a sequential conditional random layer using a gazetteer and Senna word embeddings to obtain superior performance. Magge et al. (2018) achieves state-of-the-art results in toponym detection by utilizing a window-based deep neural network, word embeddings trained on a domain-specific corpus, orthographic features, and a gazetteer.

3   Background

We briefly recap the background of several methods we include in our study.

3.1   Neural Models

Many neural approaches to natural language applications make use of in input layer that consists of tokenized text mapped to a pre-trained word embedding matrix. One common neural architecture is the deep multi-layer perceptron (MLP) which is a densely connected feed forward network with multiple layers. One or more layers of densely connected neurons are combined allowing for complex function approximation. Another common architecture, the convolutional neural network (CNN), uses mathematical cross-correlation to reduce the number of free parameters in deep models. Pooling layers can be used to combine the output of specific sets of neurons in one layer to a single neuron in a subsequent layer.

Recently, more approaches incorporate a recurrent neural network (RNN) architecture which contrasts with MLP or CNN by using internal state in subsequent processing of input sequences. A bi-LSTM is a variant of a recurrent neural network that processes sequences of input in both directions with a hidden state shared between each "step" of the sequence processing. Many deep models contain mixtures in different layers of these three architecture types.

3.2 Word Embeddings

A word embedding is a popular approach for representing text using a dense vector representation. This contrasts with traditional bag-of-word model encodings where high dimensional one-hot vectors are used to represent each words. A drawback of the bag-of-words approach is that the semantic similarity between words is lost, while dense embeddings have been shown to exhibit semantic similarity with linear relationships (Turney and Pantel, 2010).

Pre-trained embedding models can be applied as the input layer of a neural model which is then specialized for the task at hand. Mikolov et al. (2013) brought the concept of word embeddings to the forefront of natural language research with the continuous skip-gram word2vec model. This method utilizes a feedforward neural net to create a language model. The dense continuous vector representation of words in these models demonstrate superior performance on semantic word relationship tests relative to sparse term vectors. A limitation of feedforward language models including word2vec is that they are non-contextual which means that all senses of a word are merged into one dense vector.

Peters et al. (2018) propose a deep neural model (ELMo) that generates contextual word embeddings which are able to model both language and semantics of word use. ELMo embeddings assign a representation to a token as a function of the entire input token sequence. Devlin et al. (2018) introduce a pre-trained language model transformer architecture called BERT that is jointly conditioned on left and right context in all layers. The model can be fine-tuned or deep contextual embeddings can be extracted from the model layers.

4 Approach

We study three different neural approaches for toponym detection: 1) sliding windows convolutional neural networks, 2) sliding window multi-layer perceptrons, and 3) bi-LSTM. Both contextual and non-contextual word embeddings are used and enriched with a limited number of hand-crafted features. We run 5 trials for each configuration. Deep embedding variants in the analysis are: first, middle (mid), and last layer; layer concatenation (concat); weighted-average (w-avg); softmax classifier (soft) and no orthographic features (no-ortho).

We study the effects on the performance, when choosing a particular embedding (4.1) in a specialization architecture (4.3), with or without hand crafted features (4.2). The remainder of this section lays out the options we included in our study.

4.1 Embeddings

ELMo: We use deep contextual embeddings from ELMo embeddings (Peters et al., 2018) which represent learned functions of the internal states of a deep bidirectional language model that has been pre-trained on the 1B Word Benchmark (Chelba et al., 2013). In Table 2 ELMo embeddings are abbreviated as EL.

BERT: We use deep contextual embeddings generated by extracting the three uppermost layers of the model (Devlin et al., 2018) using the pre-trained BERT-Base 12-layer Cased model.[3] The BERT model uses WordPiece embeddings (Wu et al., 2016) with a 30,000 token vocabulary. We use the WordPiece embedding corresponding to the input source token and concatenate the three upper layers of the model.

w2v: The scientific-domain specific non-contextual word embeddings are provided by Pyysalo et al. (2013) which are generated from Wikipedia, PubMed, and PMC texts using the word2vec tool. They are 200-dimensional vectors trained using the skip-gram model.

For the MLP model an input embedding is generated by concatenating the ELMo vectors with the one-hot encoding of orthographic features and an additional binary encoding indicating if the token was contained within the set of gazetteer tokens. The CNN is not enhanced with either orthographic or gazetteer tokens. The bi-LSTM embedding is only enhanced with orthographic features.

---

[3]https://github.com/google-research/bert

4.2 Hand-crafted Features

Neural network based approaches have been shown to achieve strong results without the use of hand-crafted features, however, in many cases, hand-crafted features can boost model performance. We use two sets of hand-crafted features that frequently appear in the literature to increase performance in named entity recognition. In both sets of features, their inclusion did benefit performance.

Orthographic Features: a one hot encoding is assigned to each token based on its orthographic structure including presence of digits, alphabetic characters, and upper case characters. The orthographic features assist the model for managing out of vocabulary tokens.

Gazeteer Features: a set of toponynm tokens is generated from the GeoNames entries.[4] For example, for the entry in Geonames, "Gulf of Mexico", the tokens "Gulf", "of", and "Mexico" are added to the toponym set. This approach does include stop words such as "of". The impact of excluding stop words was not examined. This is used as a binary feature for the presence of the parsed token in the constructed Geonames token set. An indicator of inclusion in a gazetteer is a common feature in toponym detection models. Our study shows that this approach yields a small improvement in the MLP model performance.

4.3 Specialization Architectures

MLP: We use a sliding window multi-layer perceptron model with w2v and ELMo embeddings. A sliding window (size = 5) is applied to each tokenized sentence using the corresponding embeddings. The input layer is connected to two fully connected layers with 128 hidden units each and relu activation. The output layer uses a sigmoid with a binary output to indicate if the token is part of a toponym. MLP-EL-max is the maximum run by macro overlap F1 when using ELMo embeddings with orthographic features and gazetter indicator. MLP-w2v-max is the same model only differing by using the w2v embedding.

CNN: We use a sliding window convolutional neural network using w2v and ELMo embeddings. A sliding window (size = 5) is applied to each tokenized sentence using the corresponding embeddings. The input layer is two 1d convolutional layers with filter sizes of 250 and a kernel size

of 3. A global 1-d max pooling layer follows the convolutional layers. Two fully connected layers with 100 hidden units each and relu activation follow max pooling. A sigmoid function is applied in output layer to indicate if the token is part of a toponym. CNN-EL-max is the maximum run by macro overlap F1 when using ELMo embeddings with gazetter indicator. CNN-w2v-max is the same model only differing by using the w2v embedding.

Bi-LSTM with CRF: The implementation used is based on the approach develped by Lample et al. (2016) using code adapted from Reimers and Gurevych (2017).[5] Input sentences for the model are generated in IOB representation for labeled toponyms in the training data. Each LSTM has a size of 100 and is trained with a dropout of 0.50. Character embeddings are generated using a convolutional neural network and the maximum character length is 50. We use the w2v, ELMo and BERT embeddings for token encoding. LSTM-w2v uses w2v and orthographic features; LSTM-BERT uses BERT embeddings (top 3-layers concatenated) without orthographic features; LSTM-EL uses concatenated ELMo embeddings with orthographic features. LSTM-EL-concat-w2v is LSTM-EL embeddings concatenated with w2v.

4.4 Baseline

The following two models are included as baselines in the evaluation.

MLP-Baseline-w2v: A sliding window multi-layer perceptron as suggested by Magge et al. (2018). The system has a specific component for toponym detection using a two-layer feedforward neural network (200 hidden units per layer). The baseline features a sliding window (size = 5) over each sentence using the w2v embeddings for token encoding. The baseline did not include a gazetter-based lookup but did incorporate orthographic structure of the tokens.

TagMe: TagMe (Ferragina and Scaiella, 2010) is a state-of-the-art entity linking tool that aligns spans in text to entities in Wikipedia snapshots of April, 2016. We filter entity links to include location entities only. Spots are included as toponyms if their linked Wikipedia entity is associated with a category that contains one of the words: place, capital, province, nations, countries, territories, territory, geography, or continent

---

[4]https://www.geonames.org/export/

[5]https://github.com/UKPLab/emnlp2017-bilstm-cnn-crf

Table 1: Gold Standard Corpus Statistics.

	Documents	Tokens	Toponyms
Train	72	396,668	3,637
Valid	32	179,443	2,141
Test	45	253,159	4,616
Total	149	829,720	10,394

(TagMe-Baseline). We also run a SVM classifier that takes all categories as phrases and words. It is using LibSVM with the c-SVC algorithm and a linear kernel. The regularizer (aka "C" parameter) is tuned on the tuning split to optimize F1 and the dataset is balanced before training and tuning (TagMe-SVM).

5 Experiment Evaluation

In the following we describe our experimental evaluation using data and metrics from the SemEval Toponym resolution task.

5.1 Data

The experimental evaluation is based on a dataset of 150 full texts of open access journal articles from PubMed Central (PMC) which is provided by Davy Weissenbacher (2019).[6] To create the corpus, they convert PDF to text with the "pdf-to-text" software and then manually annotate toponym spots using the Brat annotator 3. Table 1 details statistics of this dataset.

The text documents are parsed from PDF files as many scientific articles are still not available in well-structured text formats such as XML and therefore annotators need to be adaptable to noisy inputs. The structure of the text demonstrates the challenge of using scientific text for toponym detection as the pdf-to-text conversion process results in text that introduces new line characters at non-sentence boundaries and exhibits hyphenation which splits tokens in the middle of the word. This complicates tokenization and sentence boundary detection. The pdf conversion process also injects header and footer text in the document which interrupts the flow of the documents. Tables and equations add additional noise to the text with irregular line lengths that can further complicate the extraction of toponym mentions from documents.

---

[6]From the train data set, PMC4009295.txt was not included because of encoding issues

5.2 Metrics

Quality of predictions is evaluated in terms of precision, recall and F1-measure. The model is tuned on F1 with validation on the valid set and prediction on the test set.

The dataset comes with a recommendation for two variants of evaluation: strict boundaries and overlapping boundaries. In the strict evaluation, spots must match the exact span boundaries in the gold standard. In the overlapping evaluation, a match occurs when the spot span and gold standard span overlap.

Furthermore, two options for computing precision and recall are available handling spots quality per publication. In micro-averaging all spans across the corpus treated as one set on which precision and recall is calculated. In macro averaging precision, recall, and F1 are calculated on a per publication basis, and then the results are averaged.

Over all four the evaluations measures provide similar results, we only report results on the overlapping evaluation with macro-averaging. Because the average performance of the CNN and MLP were below the average performance demonstrated by bi-LSTM, we show the maximum value of CNN and MLP to highlight that even best obtained result is less than bi-LSTM.

5.3 Results

The results are provided for precision (P), recall (P), and F1 for overlapping boundaries and macro-averages. Because of small errors in character offset alignment, the performance across all of the models for strict evaluation is slightly lower overall (omitted results will be available online).

Table 2 provides the comparison of different architectures, embeddings, and baselines.

TagMe-SVM obtains the lowest performance of all measures with a F1 of 0.330. TagMe-Baseline achieves a F1 of 0.544 and is the only model not directly trained on the data. The TagMe-SVM has a recall that is similar to that of the CNN and MLP neural methods but with a severe degradation in precision.

The ELMo embeddings enhance the F1 performance of the bi-LSTM model but appear to have limited benefit to the other studied neural models. The convolutional network using the ELMo-based embeddings exhibits higher performance on the F1 score relative to MLP-ELMo.

The CNN exhibits higher precision with similar recall to other methods that are not bi-LSTM. Bi-LSTM with CRF outperforms the MLP and CNN models independent of the embedding type. The best average performance of the bi-LSTM model is achieved when the three ELMo embeddings were concatenated, obtaining 0.910 F1. When word2vec and averaged ELMo embeddings are concatenated, a similar average F1 is achieved (0.909), however this model has the highest average precision (0.909).

Table 3 reports the results of different combinations of the ELMo embeddings based on bi-LSTM with CRF, the best performing neural model in our study. We also examine replacing the CRF classifier with a softmax when the ELMo embeddings are concatenated. The softmax classifier exhibits decreased performance with an F1 of 0.900. This indicates the importance of choosing the right classifier for the task in the bi-LSTM architecture.

We examine the effect of only using one of the three vectors provided in the ELMo embedding. In terms of average F1, the poorest performing layer is the first layer. The middle and last layer exhibit similar F1 performance. Peters et al. (2018) indicates that the lowest layer captures more syntactical information while the upper layers have a higher degree of semantic information, which may explain the performance difference in the layers.

Across all measures, the concatenation of all three ELMo vectors performed the best on average over any layer in isolation. Concatenating these three embeddings performs also slightly better than calculating an average or weighted average of the embeddings. This is based on a sample size of 5 for each measure evaluated.

Orthographic features yields an average absolute performance benefit of 2.4% in the tested MLP-w2v model. But somewhat surprisingly, causes a substantial degradation in CNN-w2v performance (-16.6% absolute). In bi-LSTM, the removal of orthographic features causes a very slight degradation in performance. This indicates that in MLP and CNN models, handcrafted features are a consideration, but may not be necessary in bi-LSTM models for toponym detection.

We also compare the performance between two contextual embeddings BERT and ELMo. Both contextual embeddings exhibit similar average F1 measures with BERT slightly underperforming ELMo. An explanatory factor could be that by

Table 2: Comparison of different architectures and embeddings.

Run	P	R	F1
TagMe-SVM	0.214	0.712	0.330
TagMe-Baseline	0.449	0.692	0.544
MLP-Baseline-w2v	0.864	0.797	0.829
MLP-EL-max	0.886	0.798	0.840
CNN-w2v-max	0.896	0.797	0.843
CNN-EL-max	0.908	0.788	0.844
MLP-w2v-max	0.888	0.835	0.861
LSTM-w2v	0.893	0.871	0.882
LSTM-BERT	0.895	0.913	0.904
LSTM-EL-concat-w2v	**0.909**	0.910	0.909
LSTM-EL-concat	0.904	**0.916**	**0.910**

only extracting the first WordPiece embedding per corresponding source token (based on the approach (Devlin et al., 2018) undertake for NER task) that information is being lost by not using all WordPiece tokens. We also use the Cased Based model, alternatively the uncased and/or Large models may yield better performance. From an implementation standpoint, the WordPiece tokenization is challenging for maintaining alignment in embedding layer composition approaches other than mapping source-to-head WordPiece token. The additional coding effort complicates the implementation of this approach.

For implementations using CNN or MLP, the results of this task did not indicate that the implementation of deep contextual embeddings yields superior performance. The appeal of non-contextual embeddings such as word2vec is their ease of implementation, which require only mapping a source token to its corresponding vector in a fixed vocabulary (or unknown if OOV). Deep contextual embeddings require mapping a token to a vector based on the "key" of its entire sentence. This is reasonable to implement but does require extra effort. The results of bi-LSTM clearly indicate that the additional performance may justify the additional implementation resources.

Figure 1 illustrates the different variations applied to the bi-LSTM with ELMo embeddings after 5 runs for each variation. Using the first layer alone in the embedding appeared to have the most negative impact on performance. Either concatenation or weighted average appear to have the most consistent highest level of performance. This is consistent with Peters et al. (2018) that found that weighted average had the best performance on a NER task using ELMo embeddings and De-

Table 3: Comparison of variations of bi-LSTM with ELMo embeddings.

Run	P	R	F1
first	0.897	0.880	0.889
soft	0.897	0.903	0.900
avg	**0.920**	0.885	0.901
last	0.896	0.912	0.904
mid	0.908	0.903	0.905
no-ortho	0.904	0.911	0.907
w-avg	0.907	0.911	0.909
concat	0.904	**0.916**	**0.910**

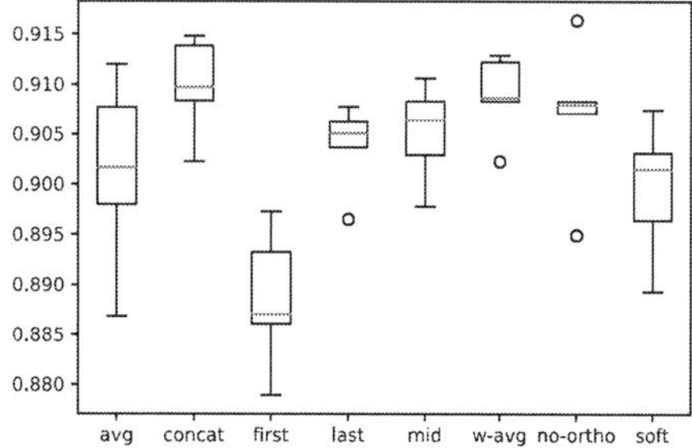

Figure 1: Comparison of variations of bi-LSTM with ELMo embeddings.

vlin et al. (2018) that found that concatenation of deep contextual embeddings (BERT) had the best performance. So either appear to be an appropriate approach given they both possess the overriding characteristic of using all layers for representation. Averaging appears to inject more variablity into performance which limits its appeal. Using softmax instead of CRF as a classifier resulted in a slight decline in performance. This highlights the importance of having a quality classifier at the top layer of the bi-LSTM for structured prediction. The omission of orthographic characters may slightly impair performance, but this is not certain, as the highest score observed out of all trials is without orthographic features (0.916). This analysis also highlights the importance of multiple trials with testing neural models as relying on one trial may sert to under or over state the average performance of a hyperparameter.

5.4 Error Analysis

Figure 2 illustrates a challenging passage of text in the corpus where none of the text should be annotated. The best performing model LSTM-EL-concat (highlighted in yellow) identifies "Britain"

The generated coordinates were then linked by the University of Portsmouth's Great Britain Historical Geographic Information System (GIS) Project to the relevant historical area boundary using county administrative diagrams (22, 23). For the 40 postcodes from 1972 (1.6%) and the 1,101 addresses from 1950 (45.0%) that could not be matched by the SAHSU team, the Great Britain Historical GIS team employed manual methods of assignment (13)

Figure 2: False positives by Tagme-Baseline and LSTM-EL-concat.

or A/Quail/Hong Kong/G1/97 (G1-like, H9N2). More importantly, some of their internal genes are closely related to those of novel H5N1 viruses isolated during the outbreak in Hong Kong in 2001.

Figure 3: False positive and false negative by Tagme-Baseline.

as a mention. While Great Britain is a place, in this context, it is highlighting a character span within an entity that is not a place. Tagme-Baseline correctly does not identify text in the prevously identified span but does incorrectly (highlighted in blue) identifies the character spans for "addresses" (a general concept not a specific location) and "Great Britain Historical GIS" (adjective for the "team" entity) as mentions. These are all examples of false positives for toponym detection.

Figure 3 shows Tagme-Baseline incorrectly identifying "Hong Kong" (highlighted in yellow) as a mention (false postive) and failing to correctly identify the second "Hong Kong" (underlined) which is an annotated mention (false negative). LSTM-EL-concat correctly did not identify the first "Hong Kong" as a mention but did properly identify the second. The first "Hong Kong" mention is part of a virus name and while has a relationship to that place it is not meant to identify the place.

6   Conclusion

In this work, we study the benefits of different neural architecture for the specialization of pre-trained embeddings for the task of toponym detection in scientific publications. We demonstrate superior results using neural models in comparison to a state-of-the-art entity linker. This indicates that general-purpose popular entity linking tools are not the optimum choice for the task. We also show that non-contextual yet domain-specific word embeddings underperform compared to deep contextual embeddings trained on a general large-scale corpus for state-of-art bi-LSTM models. We believe the increase in performance due to ELMo-based embeddings is due to the richer context and character structure contained in the embeddings. This richer representation did not benefit toponym detection in the CNN and MLP neural models tested and in fact the maximum result for MLP was using the domain specific non-contextual embedding vectors.

Out of all the neural architectures, the neural model with the best performance is bi-LSTM with CRF using concatenated ELMo contextual embeddings. This finding is consistent with other research using bi-LSTM with CRF that has demonstrated state of the art results for named entity recognition tasks. It is noteworthy, that the Bi-LSTM with CRF is able to extract toponym mentions using context from embeddings without relying on the presence of a gazetteer. An open question is if a gazetteer or other knowledge graph resources could be incorporated into a neural model to achieve superior performance.

Areas of future research include exploring the integration of dense, convolutional, or other neural architectures as a top layer of the bi-LSTM to enhance classification. Concatenating contextual and the non-contextual embeddings improved recall and incorporating both into future models could be an area that yield further performance gains.

Acknowledgements

This material is based upon work supported by the National Science Foundation under Grant No. 1846017. Any opinions, findings, and conclusions or recommendations expressed in this material are those of the author(s) and do not necessarily reflect the views of the National Science Foundation.

References

2018. Science and engineering indicators 2018. NSB-2018-1. National Science Board, Alexandria, VA.

Ciprian Chelba, Tomas Mikolov, Mike Schuster, Qi Ge, Thorsten Brants, and Phillipp Koehn. 2013. One billion word benchmark for measuring progress in statistical language modeling. *CoRR*, abs/1312.3005.

Ronan Collobert, Jason Weston, Léon Bottou, Michael Karlen, Koray Kavukcuoglu, and Pavel P. Kuksa. 2011. Natural language processing (almost) from scratch. *Journal of Machine Learning Research*, 12:2493–2537.

Karen O'Connor Matthew Scotch Graciela Gonzalez Davy Weissenbacher, Arjun Magge. 2019. Semeval-2019 task 12: Toponym resolution in scientific papers. In *Proceedings of The 13th International Workshop on Semantic Evaluation*. Association for Computational Linguistics.

Jacob Devlin, Ming-Wei Chang, Kenton Lee, and Kristina Toutanova. 2018. BERT: pre-training of deep bidirectional transformers for language understanding. *CoRR*, abs/1810.04805.

Paolo Ferragina and Ugo Scaiella. 2010. Tagme: On-the-fly annotation of short text fragments (by wikipedia entities). In *Proceedings of the 19th ACM International Conference on Information and Knowledge Management*, CIKM '10, pages 1625–1628, New York, NY, USA. ACM.

Milan Gritta, Mohammad Taher Pilehvar, Nut Limsopatham, and Nigel Collier. 2018. What's missing in geographical parsing? *Lang. Resour. Eval.*, 52(2):603–623.

Zhiheng Huang, Wei Xu, and Kai Yu. 2015. Bidirectional lstm-crf models for sequence tagging. *CoRR*, abs/1508.01991.

John D. Lafferty, Andrew McCallum, and Fernando C. N. Pereira. 2001. Conditional random fields: Probabilistic models for segmenting and labeling sequence data. In *Proceedings of the Eighteenth International Conference on Machine Learning*, ICML '01, pages 282–289.

Guillaume Lample, Miguel Ballesteros, Sandeep Subramanian, Kazuya Kawakami, and Chris Dyer. 2016. Neural architectures for named entity recognition. *CoRR*, abs/1603.01360.

Johannes Leveling. 2015. Tagging of temporal expressions and geological features in scientific articles. In *Proceedings of the 9th Workshop on Geographic Information Retrieval*, GIR '15, pages 6:1–6:10, New York, NY, USA. ACM.

Jing Li, Aixin Sun, Jianglei Han, and Chenliang Li. 2018. A survey on deep learning for named entity recognition. *CoRR*, abs/1812.09449.

Michael D. Lieberman, Hanan Samet, and Jagan Sankaranayananan. 2010. Geotagging: Using proximity, sibling, and prominence clues to understand comma groups. In *Proceedings of the 6th Workshop on Geographic Information Retrieval*, GIR '10, pages 6:1–6:8, New York, NY, USA. ACM.

Arjun Magge, Matthew Scotch, Abeed Sarker, Davy Weissenbacher, and Graciela Gonzalez-Hernandez. 2018. Deep neural networks and distant supervision for geographic location mention extraction. *Bioinformatics*, 34(13):i565–i573.

Koji Matsuda, Akira Sasaki, Naoaki Okazaki, and Kentaro Inui. 2015. Annotating geographical entities on microblog text. In *Proceedings of The 9th Linguistic*

Annotation Workshop, pages 85–94. Association for Computational Linguistics.

Tomas Mikolov, Kai Chen, Greg Corrado, and Jeffrey Dean. 2013. Efficient estimation of word representations in vector space. *CoRR*, abs/1301.3781.

Matthew E. Peters, Mark Neumann, Mohit Iyyer, Matt Gardner, Christopher Clark, Kenton Lee, and Luke Zettlemoyer. 2018. Deep contextualized word representations. *CoRR*, abs/1802.05365.

Jakub Piskorski and Roman Yangarber. 2013. Information extraction: Past, present and future. In Thierry Poibeau, Horacio Saggion, Jakub Piskorski, and Roman Yangarber, editors, *Multi-source, Multilingual Information Extraction and Summarization*, Theory and Applications of Natural Language Processing, pages 23–49. Springer Berlin Heidelberg.

Sampo Pyysalo, Filip Ginter, Hans Moen, Tapio Salakoski, and Sophia Ananiadou. 2013. Distributional semantics resources for biomedical text processing.

Nils Reimers and Iryna Gurevych. 2017. Reporting Score Distributions Makes a Difference: Performance Study of LSTM-networks for Sequence Tagging. In *Proceedings of the 2017 Conference on Empirical Methods in Natural Language Processing (EMNLP)*, pages 338–348, Copenhagen, Denmark.

Francesco Ronzano and Horacio Saggion. 2016. Knowledge extraction and modeling from scientific publications. In *Semantics, Analytics, Visualization. Enhancing Scholarly Data*, pages 11–25, Cham. Springer International Publishing.

W. Shen, J. Wang, and J. Han. 2015. Entity linking with a knowledge base: Issues, techniques, and solutions. *IEEE Transactions on Knowledge & Data Engineering*, 27(2):443–460.

Peter D. Turney and Patrick Pantel. 2010. From frequency to meaning: Vector space models of semantics. *CoRR*, abs/1003.1141.

Davy Weissenbacher, Tasnia Tahsin, Rachel Beard, Mari Figaro, Robert Rivera, Matthew Scotch, and Graciela Gonzalez. 2015. Knowledge-driven geospatial location resolution for phylogeographic models of virus migration. *Bioinformatics*, 31(12):i348–i356. Exported from https://app.dimensions.ai on 2019/03/04.

Yonghui Wu, Mike Schuster, Zhifeng Chen, Quoc V. Le, Mohammad Norouzi, Wolfgang Macherey, Maxim Krikun, Yuan Cao, Qin Gao, Klaus Macherey, Jeff Klingner, Apurva Shah, Melvin Johnson, Xiaobing Liu, Lukasz Kaiser, Stephan Gouws, Yoshikiyo Kato, Taku Kudo, Hideto Kazawa, Keith Stevens, George Kurian, Nishant Patil, Wei Wang, Cliff Young, Jason Smith, Jason Riesa, Alex Rudnick, Oriol Vinyals, Greg Corrado, Macduff Hughes, and Jeffrey Dean. 2016. Google's neural machine translation system: Bridging the gap between human and machine translation. *CoRR*, abs/1609.08144.

Juan Zhang, Jun Xie, Wanli Hou, Xiaochen Tu, Jing Xu, Fujian Song, Zhihong Wang, and Zuxun Lu. 2012. Mapping the knowledge structure of research on patient adherence: Knowledge domain visualization based co-word analysis and social network analysis. *PLOS ONE*, 7(4):1–7.

STAC: Science Toolkit Based on Chinese Idiom Knowledge Graph

Meiling Wang[1], Min Xiao[2], Changliang Li[1*], Yu Guo[1], Zhixin Zhao[1] and Xiaonan Liu[1]
[1]AI Lab, KingSoft Corp, Beijing, China
[2]Beijing University of Posts and Telecommunications, Beijing, China
{wangmeiling1, lichangliang, guoyu9}@kingsoft.com
{zhaozhixin, liuxiaonan1}@kingsoft.com
xiaomincloud@gmail.com

Abstract

Chinese idioms (Cheng Yu) have seen five t-housand years' history and culture of China, meanwhile they contain large number of scientific achievement of ancient China. However, existing Chinese online idiom dictionaries have limited function for scientific exploration. In this paper, we first construct a Chinese idiom knowledge graph by extracting domains and dynasties and associating them with idioms, and based on the idiom knowledge graph, we propose a Science Toolkit for Ancient China (STAC) aiming to support scientific exploration. In the STAC toolkit, idiom navigator helps users explore overall scientific progress from idiom perspective with visualization tools, and idiom card and idiom QA shorten action path and avoid thinking being interrupted while users are reading and writing. The current STAC toolkit is deployed at http://120.92.208.22:7476/demo/#/stac.

1 Introduction

Large scientific wealth has been accumulated during five thousand years' history of ancient China, and much knowledge passed down from ancients is still valuable for modern people, therefore lots of researchers are exploring ancient Chinese science and technology (Jia et al., 2004; Zhu et al., 1998b,a) continuously.

Chinese idioms (Cheng Yu) have seen the history and culture of China, meanwhile they contain large number of scientific achievement of ancient China (Dai, 2003). For the example in Table 1, "一寸光阴一寸金" (One inch of time, one inch of gold) mentions time measurement technique using sundial of ancient Astronomy domain in Han dynasty (汉朝). Therefore, Chinese idioms are regarded as an important source of ancient scientific achievement information. However, existing Chinese online idiom dictionaries, such as Baidu

Chinese Channel[1], Han dictionary[2] and Cihai online dictionaries[3], have limited function for scientific exploration. Those online idiom dictionaries mainly store basic information of idioms, e.g., pronunciation, explanation, source, synonyms and antonyms, and they can be leveraged to search idioms by names or keywords and to get basic information of idioms, but it is difficult for researchers to get idioms by domain and dynasty information, and it is also impossible to obtain the trend of scientific progress from idiom perspective.

In this paper, we propose a Science Toolkit for Ancient China (STAC) based on a Chinese idiom knowledge graph aiming to support scientific exploration. We first extract domains and dynasties from explanation and source of idioms, and then associate domains and dynasties with idioms to construct the idiom knowledge graph. Based on the knowledge graph, we design and implement idiom navigator, idiom card and idiom QA of S-TAC toolkit. Idiom navigator provides a visual presentation for relations among idioms, dynasties and domains, reflecting overall scientific progress from idiom perspective, and idiom card gives basic information of idioms contained in users' text, such as dynasty, domain, explanation and source, and idiom QA answers idioms to questions about dynasties and domains, such as "宋代的天文领域成语" (The idioms on Astronomy domain in Song dynasty). Both idiom card and idiom QA are designed for scenarios of text reading and writing to shorten the path of users' actions and avoid users' thinking being interrupted.

2 Dataset

We mainly collect idiom data from Han dictionary and Baidu Chinese Channel, and Han dictionary

---

[1]https://dict.baidu.com/
[2]www.zdic.net
[3]For example, http://www.cihai123.com/

Proceedings of the Workshop on Extracting Structured Knowledge from Scientific Publications, pages 57–61
Minneapolis, USA, June 6, 2019. ©2019 Association for Computational Linguistics

Name	一寸光阴一寸金 (One inch of time, one inch of gold)
Explanation	一寸光阴和一寸长的黄金一样昂贵，其中"一寸光阴"是指晷针的影子在晷盘上移动一寸距离所使用的时间。(One inch of time is as expensive as one inch of gold, where "one inch of time" refers to time taking by shadow of gnomon to move one inch distance on sundial plate.)
Source	刘安所著《淮南子》 ("Huai Nan Zi" of Liu An)
Domain	天文 (Astronomy)
Dynasty	汉朝 (Han dynasty)

Table 1: An example of Chinese idioms.

is the most reliable and Baidu Chinese is much more comprehensive. Firstly, we get 31,605 idioms from Han dictionary and 30,923 idioms from Baidu Chinese Channel respectively, and properties of these idioms include pronunciation, explanation and source. Then we merge the two idiom sets by setting Han dictionary prior to Baidu dictionary for the duplicate idioms. The final dataset is stored in MySQL database, containing 31,632 idioms, whose average number of characters in explanation is 24 and average number of characters in source is 32.

3   Idiom Knowledge Graph (IKG) Construction

We construct an idiom knowledge graph based on the dataset collected in Section 2. Hereinafter the idiom knowledge graph is referred to as IKG. The ontology definition of IKG contains:

(1) three types of entities, which are idiom entity denoted as $IDIOM$, dynasty entity denoted as $DYNASTY$, and domain entity denoted as $DOMAIN$;

(2) three types of properties, which are explanation of idiom denoted as $explanation\_of$, source of idiom denoted as $source\_of$, and pronunciation of idiom denoted as $pronunciation\_of$;

(3) two types of relations, which are relation between dynasties and idioms denoted as $dynasty\_of$, and relation between domains and idioms denoted as $domain\_of$.

Instances of $IDIOM$ are selected from 31,632 idioms of the dataset in relation extraction process, and instances of $explanation\_of$, $source\_of$ and $pronunciation\_of$ are queried directly from the dataset. There are 14 $DYNASTY$ instances, which are defined according to the main dynasties of ancient Chinese history, such as "战国" (War-ring), "汉" (Han) and "宋" (Song), and there are 11 $DOMAIN$ instances, which almost cover all the domains in ancient China, such as "天文" (Astronomy), "手工业" (Handicraft) and "医药" (Medicine).

The relation extraction process of $domain\_of$ and $dynasty\_of$ is divided into following steps as shown in Figure 1:

(1) For each idiom in the dataset, concat its explanation string and source string and tokenize the result string into a word bag with jieba tool[4], and then for each word in the word bag, add its hypernym and hyponym words from semantic dictionaries (e.g., HowNet[5]) into the word bag, until the word bag is no longer changing in its size, and the result word bag is used as a feature of the idiom.

(2) Load a Chinese word vectors corpus pretrained on Chinese Wikipedia and Baidu Encyclopedia (Li et al., 2018), and then embeddings of 31,632 idioms, 14 $DYNASTY$ instances and 11 $DOMAIN$ instances can be looked up from it.

(3) Compute correlation based on WMD (Word Mover's Distance) algorithm (Kusner et al., 2015) that can achieve better results for short texts, and confirm final relations by human reviewers:

- for each $DOMAIN$ instance, compute its correlation with all the idioms, and send top 100 idioms for human review to confirm final instances of $domain\_of$ relation;

---

[4]https://github.com/fxsjy/jieba
[5]http://www.keenage.com/zhiwang/c_zhiwang.html

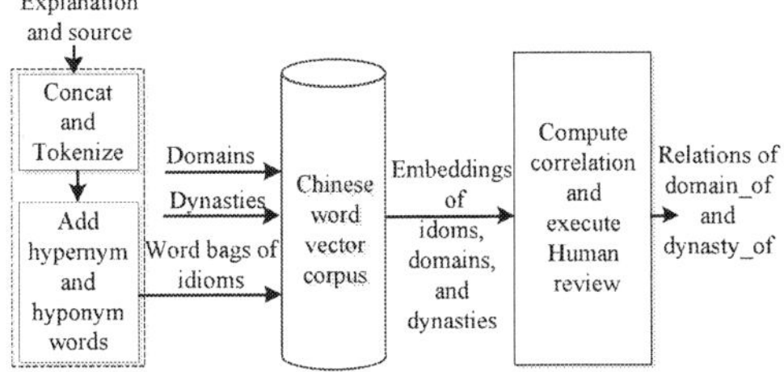

Figure 1: Relation extraction framework of IKG.

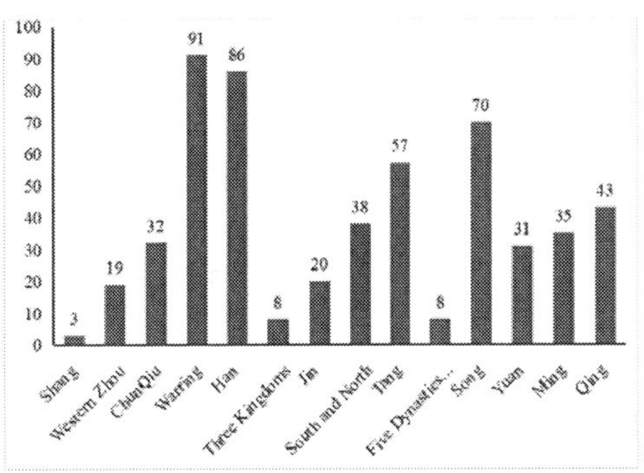

(a) Distribution of *IDIOM* instances across *DYNASTY* instances.

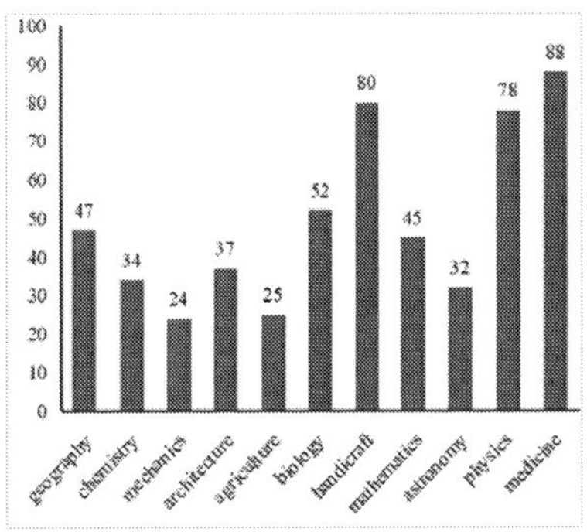

(b) Distribution of *IDIOM* instances across *DOMAIN* instances.

Figure 2: Distribution of *IDIOM* instances across *DYNASTY* instances and *DOMAIN* instances.

- for each idiom, compute its correlation with all the *DYNASTY* instances and send top 3 *DYNASTY* entities for human review to confirm final instances of *dynasty_of* relation, and human reviewers could make decision with information of books and authors contained in source text, e.g., "Huai Nan Zi" (《淮南子》) and "Liu An" (刘安) in Table 1.

Finally, 542 instances of *domain_of* relation are extracted and 532 *IDIOM* instances are selected from the 31,632 idioms, and for the 532 *IDIOM* instances, 541 instances of *dynasty_of* relation are extracted. The whole knowledge graph is stored in Neo4j[6] graph database.

Figure 2 describes some statistics about IKG. From Figure 2(a), we can see that the scientific progress in "战国" (Warring), "汉" (Han) and "宋" (Song) is more significant than in other dynasties, and from Figure 2(b), we can see that the scientific progress in "医药" (Medicine), "手工业"(Handicraft) and "物理" (Physics) is more significant than in other domains.

4 STAC Toolkit

Based on IKG, we design and implement STAC toolkit for scientific exploration of ancient China, and the toolkit contains functions of idiom navigator, idiom card and idiom QA.

4.1 Idiom navigator

Idiom navigator is an idiom visualization tool, and it gets all the idioms, dynasties and domains from IKG and organizes them in tree structures based on the relations contained in IKG. With idiom navigator, users can browse idioms starting from dynasties or domains. For example, after selecting each dynasty, users can get expanded all the domains that were developed in the dynasty, and af-

ter selecting one of these domains, they can also get expanded all the idioms related with both the domain and the dynasty. Then users could gain information on scientific progress level from idiom perspective.

4.2 Idiom card

Idiom card provides basic information for the idioms contained in users' text, and users do not need to switch to online idiom dictionaries, therefore the action path to get information of idioms is shortened and users' thinking is not interrupted.

Given a piece of text, we first extract all the idioms from the text by multi-pattern matching algorithm (e.g., Aho-Corasick string match algorithm (Aho and Corasick, 1975)), and then for each idiom extracted, we query its dynasty, domain, explanation, source and pronunciation from IKG. In detail, domain and dynasty are queried by relations, and explanation, source and pronunciation are queried by properties. Finally, queried results for all the idioms are presented to users.

---

[6]https://neo4j.com/

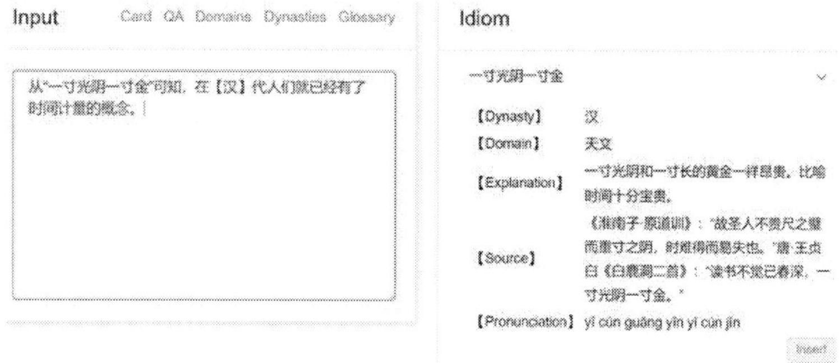

Figure 3: Snapshot of STAC toolkit landing page.

4.3 Idiom QA

For questions about dynasties and domains, idiom QA gives corresponding accurate idioms as answer.

Given a question, we first extract all the dynasties and domains from the question by multi-pattern matching algorithm, and then we construct a query statement using the extracted dynasties and domains and execute the statement on IKG to get idioms. In detail, the query statement is constructed as "select all the idioms that are associated with all the dynasties and domains". Finally, queried idioms are presented to users.

4.4 Deployment

STAC toolkit is developed using Django[7] web framework as backend, Neo4j as graph database and Vue.js JavaScript library[8] for frontend page rendering, and we implement visualization of idiom navigator with Zoomcharts.js library[9]. STAC toolkit is currently accessible at http://120.92.208.22:7476/demo/#/stac with Google Chrome browser (Please note that the first visit may take about 60 seconds). Figure 3 shows a snapshot of STAC toolkit landing page.

We are continuously improving STAC toolkit, and currently, users can use it in the following way:

(1) Call out idiom navigator visualization tool by clicking button "Domains" or "Dynasties", and double-click nodes of type *DOMAIN* or *DYNASTY* to expand related nodes until reaching end. Please note that some nodes of *DOMAIN* or *DYNASTY* cannot be expanded because there are no related nodes under them.

(2) Input some text into the left "Input" area, and get card for idioms contained in text by clicking button "Card". For example, input "从'一寸光阴一寸金'可知..." (From the idiom "One inch of time, one inch of gold" we can see that...) and the idiom card of "一寸光阴一寸金" is displayed in the right "Idiom" area, containing its dynasty, domain, explanation, source and pronunciation.

(3) Call out QA dialog box by clicking button "QA", and then enter some question about dynasties and domains (e.g., the question example in Section 1), and finally click "OK" button to get idioms as answer. Meanwhile idioms in answer could be inserted into text by clicking button "Insert". Please note that dynasties and domains in questions are assumed to be correct, and similar words are not supported for questions.

(4) Call out glossary window by clicking button "Glossary", and then read the Chinese-English glossary of dynasties and domains.

5 Conclusion

In this paper, we first construct a Chinese idiom knowledge graph and then propose STAC toolkit that contains functions of idiom navigator, idiom card and idiom QA for scientific exploration. Currently, idiom navigator helps users explore overall scientific progress from idiom perspective, and idiom card and idiom QA shorten action path and avoid thinking being interrupted while users are reading and writing. In future, we plan to improve idiom QA by context understanding and conduct more evaluations on the idiom knowledge graph and STAC.

---

[7]https://www.djangoproject.com/
[8]https://vuejs.org/
[9]https://zoomcharts.com/

References

Alfred V Aho and Margaret J Corasick. 1975. Efficient string matching: an aid to bibliographic search. *Communications of the ACM*, 18(6):333–340.

Wusan Dai. 2003. *Ancient Technology in Idioms.* Baihua Literature and Art Publishing House, Tijin, China.

Wei Jia, Wenyuan Gao, Yongqing Yan, Jie Wang, Zhaohui Xu, Wenjie Zheng, and Peigen Xiao. 2004. The rediscovery of ancient chinese herbal formulas. *Phytotherapy Research: An International Journal Devoted to Pharmacological and Toxicological Evaluation of Natural Product Derivatives*, 18(8):681–686.

Matt Kusner, Yu Sun, Nicholas Kolkin, and Kilian Weinberger. 2015. From word embeddings to document distances. In *Proceedings of the 32nd International Conference on Machine Learning*, pages 957–966.

Shen Li, Zhe Zhao, Renfen Hu, Wensi Li, Tao Liu, and Xiaoyong Du. 2018. Analogical reasoning on chinese morphological and semantic relations. In *Proceedings of the 56th Annual Meeting of the Association for Computational Linguistics (Volume 2: Short Papers)*, pages 138–143. Association for Computational Linguistics.

Jiashi Zhu, Georges M Halpern, and Kenneth Jones. 1998a. The scientific rediscovery of a precious ancient chinese herbal regimen: Cordyceps sinensis part ii. *The Journal of Alternative and Complementary Medicine*, 4(4):429–457.

Jiashi Zhu, Georges M Halpern, and Kenneth Jones. 1998b. The scientific rediscovery of an ancient chinese herbal medicine: Cordyceps sinensis part i. *The Journal of alternative and complementary medicine*, 4(3):289–303.

Playing by the Book: An Interactive Game Approach for Action Graph Extraction from Text

Ronen Tamari*
The Hebrew University of Jerusalem
`ronent@cs.huji.ac.il`

Hiroyuki Shindo
NAIST / RIKEN-AIP
`shindo@is.naist.jp`

Dafna Shahaf
The Hebrew University of Jerusalem
`dshahaf@cs.huji.ac.il`

Yuji Matsumoto
NAIST / RIKEN-AIP
`matsu@is.naist.jp`

Abstract

Understanding procedural text requires tracking entities, actions and effects as the narrative unfolds. We focus on the challenging real-world problem of action-graph extraction from *materials science* papers, where language is highly specialized and data annotation is expensive and scarce. We propose a novel approach, TEXT2QUEST, where procedural text is interpreted as instructions for an *interactive game*. A learning agent completes the game by executing the procedure correctly in a text-based simulated lab environment. The framework can complement existing approaches and enables richer forms of learning compared to static texts. We discuss potential limitations and advantages of the approach, and release a prototype proof-of-concept, hoping to encourage research in this direction.

1 Introduction

Materials science literature includes a vast amount of synthesis procedures described in natural language. The ability to automatically parse these texts into a structured form could allow for data-driven synthesis planning, a key enabler in the design and discovery of novel materials (Kim et al., 2018; Mysore et al., 2017). A particularly useful parsing is **action graph extraction**, which maps a passage describing a procedure to a symbolic action-graph representation of the core entities, operations and their accompanying arguments, as they unfold throughout the text (Fig. 1).

Procedural text understanding is a highly challenging task for today's learning algorithms (Lucy and Gauthier, 2017; Levy et al., 2017). Synthesis procedures are especially challenging, as they are written in difficult and highly technical language assuming prior knowledge. Some texts are long,

many follow a non-linear narrative, or include logical quantifiers ("all synthesis steps were performed in an argon atmosphere..."). Furthermore, annotated data is scarce and expensive to obtain.

Two related research areas are **grounded semantic parsing** and **state-tracking reading-comprehension**. Grounded (or executable) semantic parsers map natural language to a symbolic representation which can also be thought of as a sequence of instructions in some pre-defined programming language. Such "neural-programing" architectures offer strong symbolic reasoning capabilities, compositionality modelling, and strong generalization (Reed and de Freitas, 2015), but are typically applied to simple texts due to prohibitive annotation costs (Liang et al., 2016). **State-tracking** models (Bosselut et al., 2018; Das et al., 2018; Bansal et al., 2017) can model complex relations between entities as they unfold, with easier training but less symbolic reasoning abilities. Their applicability to longer texts is hindered as well by the lack of fine-grained annotated data.

In this work we describe an approach, TEXT2QUEST, that attempts to combine the strengths of both methods. Instead of trying to learn from static text, we propose to treat procedural text as **instructions for an interactive game** (or "quest"). The learning agent interacts with entities defined in the text by executing symbolic actions (Fig. 2). A text-based symbolic interpreter handles execution and tracking of the agent's state and actions. The game is completed by "simulating" the instructions correctly; i.e., mapping instructions to a sequence of actions. Correct simulation thus directly yields the desired action graph.

While there is some engineering overhead required for the simulator, we demonstrate that it is relatively straightforward to convert an annotation schema to a text-based game. We believe that the benefits make it worth pursuing: the game for-

---

*Work was begun while author was an intern at RIKEN and continued at the Hebrew University.

Proceedings of the Workshop on Extracting Structured Knowledge from Scientific Publications, pages 62–71
Minneapolis, USA, June 6, 2019. ©2019 Association for Computational Linguistics

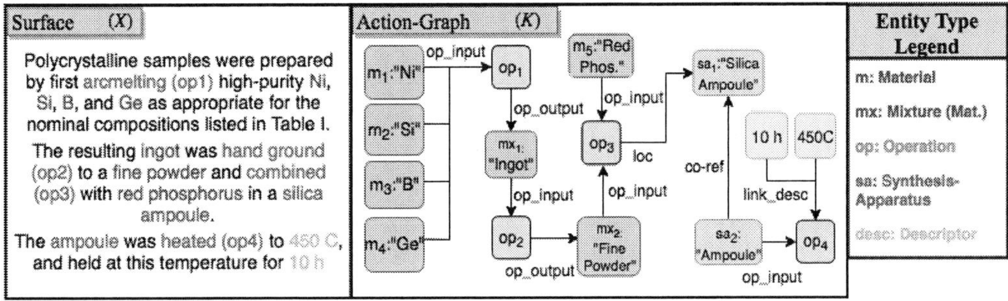

Figure 1: Sample surface text (left) and possible corresponding action-graph (right) for typical partial material synthesis procedure. Operation numbers in parentheses are added for clarity. Nodes are entities, edges are relations linking them, equivalent to actions in the text-based game.

mat allows applying powerful neural programming methods, with a significantly richer training environment, including advances such as curriculum learning, common-sense and domain-specific constraints, and full state tracking. Such "friendly" environments that assist the learning agent have been shown to be valuable (Liang et al., 2016) and enable learning of patterns that are often hard to learn from surface annotations alone, such as implicit effects of operations (i.e., filtering a mixture splits it into two entities).

Interestingly, understanding by simulation aligns well with models of human cognition; mental simulation, the ability to construct and manipulate an internal world model, is a cornerstone of human intelligence involved in many unique behaviors, including language comprehension (Marblestone et al., 2016; Hamrick, 2019). In this work we take first steps towards this idea. Our contributions are:

- We propose a **novel formulation** of the problem of procedural text understanding as a text-based game, enabling the use of neural programming and text-based reinforcement learning (RL) methods.
- We present and release TEXTLABS[1], an instance of TEXT2QUEST designed for interaction with synthesis procedure texts. We focus on the material-science setting, but the approach is intended to be more generally applicable.
- We propose to address the problem of obtaining full-graph annotations at scale by coupling the simulator with **controllable natural language generation** (NLG) to generate synthetic data, also enabling curriculum learning.

---

[1] Code and experiments available at `https://github.com/ronentk/TextLabs`

The starting materials are nickel and zinc. First, grind the materials. After that, mix, heat and compact them.
You are in the Lab.
Available operations are: a grind_op, a heat_op and a mix_op.
Available materials are: nickel and zinc.
> *input_assign nickel to grind_op*
Input assigned!
> *input_assign zinc to grind_op*
Input assigned!
> *run grind_op*
Ground materials!
> *Examine grind_op's output*
The grind_op's output is a mixture. It contains nickel and zinc. It is powder.

Figure 2: Excerpt from an actual "material synthesis quest" generated by our system with example input/outputs.

While this work is preliminary in nature, neural programming and text-based reinforcement learning approaches are attracting significant and growing interest, and we expect advances in these areas to directly benefit future versions of the system.

2 Related Work

Procedure understanding: Many recent works have focused on tracking entities and relations in long texts, such as cooking recipes and scientific processes (Bosselut et al., 2018; Das et al., 2018). However, these methods do not directly extract a full action graph. For action graph extraction, earlier works use sequence tagging methods (Mysore et al., 2017). Feng et al. (2018) have applied deep-RL to the problem of extracting action sequences, but assume explicit procedural instruction texts. In Johnson (2017), a graph is constructed from simple generated stories, using state tracking at each time step as supervision.

Semantic parsing & Neural Programming: Research to-date has focused mainly on shorter and simpler texts which may require complex symbolic reasoning, such as mapping natural language to queries over knowledge graphs (Liang et al., 2016). In the case of narrative parsing, the text itself may be complex while the programs are relatively simple (creating and linking between entities present in the text). Recent work (Lu et al., 2018) frames narrative understanding as neural-programming, the learner converts a document into a structured form, using a predefined set of data-structures. This approach is similar to ours, though with simpler texts and without a simulated environment. In our approach, the learning architecture is decoupled from the symbolic interpreter environment, enabling greater architectural flexibility.

Text-RL: Text-based games are used to study language grounding and understanding and RL for combinatorical action spaces (Zahavy et al., 2018; Narasimhan, 2017) but have not yet been applied to real world problems. TextWorld (Côté et al., 2018) is a recently released reinforcement learning sandbox environment for creation of custom text-based games, upon which we base TEXTLABS.

3 Problem Formulation

Entities, Relations & Rules $(\mathcal{E}, \mathcal{R}, \Lambda)$: Assume two vocabularies defining types of *entities* $\mathcal{E} = \{e_1, ..., e_N\}$ and *relations* $\mathcal{R} = \{r_1, ..., r_K\}$. A *fact* f is a grounded predicate of the form $f = r(h, t)$, $h, t \in \mathcal{E}$, $r \in \mathcal{R}$ (single or double argument predicate relations are allowed). We define the set of valid world-states S, where a state $s \in S$ is a set of facts, and validity is decided by a world-model Λ defined using linear logic. Λ is comprised of production rules (or transition rules) over entities and relations governing which new facts can be produced from a given state. Following the schema used in the Synthesis Project[2] (see for example MSP), entity types include materials, operations, and relevant descriptors (like operation conditions, etc.). Relations link between entities (like *input(material,operation)* or denote single predicate relations (entity properties such as *solid(material)*). We currently use a simplified version of the schema to ease the learning problem. See appendix A.1 for a mapping of relations and entities. Production rules correspond to the actions available to the learner, in our domain these include for example *link-descriptor(descriptor,entity)*, *input-assign(material, operation)*. While not currently

---

[2]https://www.synthesisproject.org/

included, actions such as co-reference linking and generation of entities can also be incorporated.

Action-Graph (K): An action sequence is defined to be a sequence of valid actions (or production rules) rooted at some initial state s_0: $K = (s_0, \lambda_0, \lambda_1, ..., \lambda_n)$ (applying λ_i to s_i results in s_{i+1}, intermediate states are left out for brevity). Note that actions may apply to implicit entities not present in the surface text (for example, the result of an operation). Construction of an action graph corresponding to K is straightforward (entities as nodes, actions connecting them as edges), and henceforth we use K to denote either the sequence or the graph. Note that there can be multiple possible action sequences resulting in the same action graph, equivalent w.r.t the topological ordering of operations induced by their dependencies.

Surface (X): A *surface* is simply a text in natural language describing a process.

Learning Task: Our objective is to learn a mapping $\Psi : X \to K$. As this mapping may be highly complex, we convert the problem to a structured prediction setting. As an intermediate step **we map an input X to an enriched text-based-game G representation** (details below), where the solution of G is the required action graph K. The game is modelled as a partially observable Markov Decision Process (POMDP) $G = (S, A, T, \Omega, O, R, \gamma)$.

We refer the reader to Côté et al. (2018) for a detailed exposition, and focus here on mapping the game-setting to our approach: S are states, A are actions, T are conditional state transition probabilities, where all are constant per domain and defined by $\mathcal{E}, \mathcal{R}, \Lambda$. Ω are observations, and O are conditional observations probabilities. $R : S \times A \to \mathbb{R}$ is the reward function, $\gamma \in [0, 1]$ is the discount factor. As γ, Ω, O are also preset (with actual observations dependent on agent actions), mapping a surface X to game G boils down to providing a list of entities for initializing s_0. For training and evaluation, a reward function must also be provided (not necessary for applying a trained model on un-annotated text "in the wild").

If a fully annotated action graph is available (whether synthetic or real), this mapping is simple: the initial game state s_0 is a room where the agent is placed alongside all entities. Each edge corresponds to an action in the game. Given an action sequence K, a reward function R can be automatically computed, giving intermediate rewards and penalizing wrong actions. A quest in TextWorld can be defined via a final goal state, thus allowing

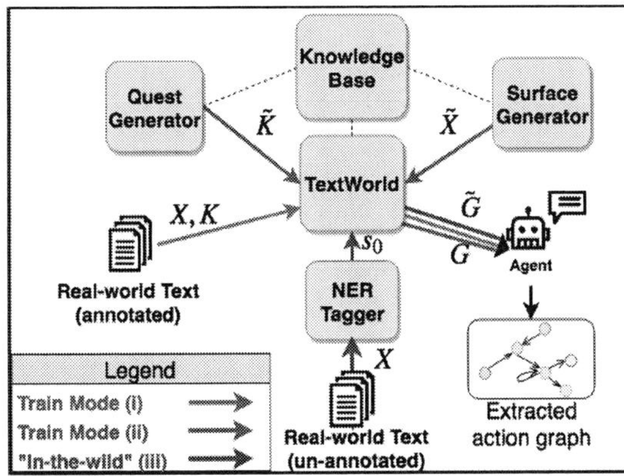

Figure 3: Proposed solution architecture of TEXT2QUEST. (i) Flow for training agent on games from real annotated data. (ii) Flow for training agent on synthetic games. (iii) Extracting action graph from un-annotated real data.

multiple possible winning action sequences. See appendices A.2, A.3 for examples.

For data "in the wild", entities can be identified using named entity recognition (NER) as pre-processing. Future directions include end-to-end learning to reduce cascading initialization errors.

By default, the TextWorld environment is partially observable. The agent observes the surface X at time $t = 0$ and other textual descriptions upon executing an "examine" action. Unlike classic text-based games where partial observability is part of the challenge, in our case we can adopt the "friendly-environment" perspective and assist the learner with information such as state-tracking or action pruning (Liang et al., 2016; Johnson, 2017).

4 Proposed Solution Architecture

Our system consists of 6 core modules (Fig. 3): a Knowledge Base defines entity, relation and action vocabularies. This is used by the Surface Generator and Quest Generator modules to generate pairs $(\tilde{X}, \tilde{K})$ of synthetic surfaces and their corresponding action graphs for training. For un-annotated text, a pre-trained domain specific NER tagger[3] is used to extract an initial game state s_0 by identifying the mentioned entities. A learning agent extracts K from a generated game.

The TEXT2QUEST architecture supports three central modes of operation: (i) Enrich existing real world annotated pairs (X, K) by converting them

to game instances for training the game-solving agent. (ii) Produce synthetic training pairs $(\tilde{X}, \tilde{K})$. (iii) Convert un-annotated texts to game instances for action graph extraction "in the wild".

The current version of TEXTLABS supports mode (ii). We implemented simple prototypes of the domain-specific Knowledge Base, plus Quest and Surface Generators. See Sec. A.1 for details about converting the entity and relation annotation schema into TextWorld. TextWorld is easily extensible and can support a variety of interaction semantics. Aside from adding a domain specific entity type-tree and actions, most of the underlying logic engine and interface is handled automatically. For the game environment, we use Inform7, a programming language and interpreter for text-based games. For quest generation, we currently use simple forward chaining and heuristic search strategies to create plausible quests (for example, all start materials must be incorporated into the synthesis route). Combining these with a simple rule-based Surface Generator already allows for creating simple synthetic training game instances (Fig. 2).

5 Preliminary Evaluation

As a very preliminary sanity check for the TEXTLABS environment, we train a simple text-based RL agent on synthetic games in increasingly difficult environments. Difficulty is measured by maximum quest length, and the number of entities in the target action graph. See Sec. A.2 for representative examples. We use the basic LSTM-DQN agent of Narasimhan (2017) adapted to the TEXTLABS setting. The action space is $A = \{W_v \times W_{o_1} \times W_{o_2}\}$, where W_v consists of 8 action-verbs corresponding to the entity relations tracked and additional native TextWorld actions like *take* (see Sec. A.1 for details). W_{o_1}, W_{o_2} are (identical) sets of potential arguments corresponding to the active entities which can be interacted with in the game (single and double argument actions allowed). As this basic agent is not conditioned on previous actions, we further concatenate the last four commands taken to the current observation. For the same reason, we also append the full quest instructions at every timestep's observation. All illegal actions are pruned at each state to reduce search space size.

We train the agent on 100 games per level and test on 10 games. Evaluation is measured by avg. normalized reward per game: $\frac{1}{|K|} \sum_{t=1}^{T} r_i$, where K is the true action sequence, T is the episode

---

[3]For the materials synthesis domain we use the tagger available at `https://github.com/olivettigroup/materials-synthesis-generative-models`

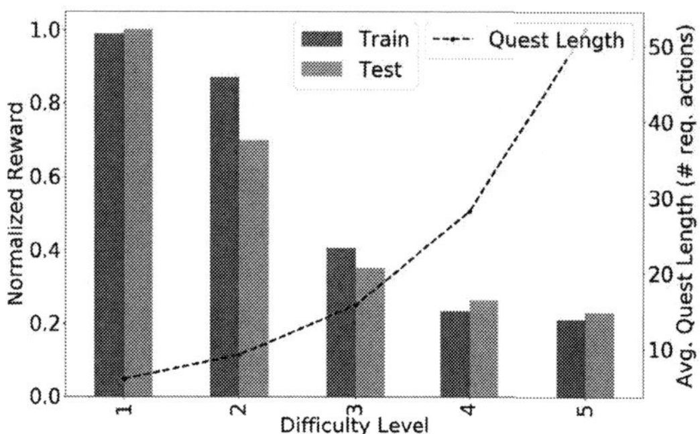

Figure 4: Preliminary evaluation results for a basic LSTM-DQN text-RL agent on synthetic quests. Dotted line shows average generated quest lengths.

length (set to 50) and $r_i = 1$ for each action in K and -1 for otherwise (and 0 for neutral actions like *examine*). A normalized score of 1 means the agent performed the required actions exactly.

As can be seen in Fig. 4, the agent learns to successfully perform the required actions only for the easiest levels. Examining longer games the agent did not complete, we note that the lack of conditioning on previous states is a serious limitation. Equipping agents with better sequence encoding (e.g., attention), recurrent memory, and utilizing state information is expected to significantly improve performance. Furthermore, due to technical limitations of the current implementation, some actions cannot be reversed. This adds to the difficulty of the task, and will be addressed in future versions. Finally, learning good initial policies for semantic parsers is known to be a hard problem with RL alone, and related approaches commonly use hybrid RL/supervised training methods (Liang et al., 2016; Jiang et al., 2012).

6 Discussion

Our approach faces tough challenges. However, we are encouraged by the significant recent advances towards these challenges in related areas, and plan to leverage this progress for our framework.

Programming semantics and rewards for instruction-following agents is known to be notoriously difficult (Winograd, 1972) as language and environments grow increasingly complex. Research on **learned instruction-conditional reward models** (Bahdanau et al., 2018) is a promising approach towards reducing the amount of "environment engineering" required.

Another critical open question in our framework is whether the surface generator will be able to generate surfaces representative enough to allow for generalization to real examples. Current NLG systems are increasingly capable of structured text generation (Marcheggiani and Perez, 2018), and though they produce relatively short surfaces, we believe that coupling them with the generated action graphs is a promising approach to scaling up to longer sequences while maintaining coherence. Such systems can use sentence-level semantic parses as training data, meaning they can leverage existing weakly-supervised shallow parsing techniques. Encouraging for our modelling paradigm, recent work (Peng et al., 2018) extending the Dyna-Q (DQ) framework (Sutton, 1990) demonstrates a real-world application of structured NLG with a simulated RL training environment.

Given sufficient text generation capabilities, one may question the added utility of the game environment (as opposed to learning a direct mapping $X \rightarrow K$). Recent research suggests that for stronger generalization, data alone may not be enough, and symbolic reasoning capabilities are necessary (Khashabi et al., 2018; Yi et al., 2018). Given the compositional complexity and difficulty of the language involved, we believe they will prove necessary in our setting as well.

7 Conclusions

There is a growing need for combining neuro-symbolic reasoning with advanced language representation methods. In the case of procedural text understanding, key obstacles are suitable training environments, as well as the lack of fully annotated action graphs. Motivated by this, we proposed TEXT2QUEST, an approach intended to enhance learning by turning raw text inputs into a structured *text-based game* environment, as well as augmenting data with synthetic fully annotated action graphs. To encourage further research in this direction, we publicly release TEXTLABS, an instance of TEXT2QUEST for the materials synthesis task. We implemented prototype modules for basic game generation and solving. Future work will focus on designing learning agents to solve the games, as well as improving text generation capabilities. We hope that the proposed approach will lead to developing useful systems for action graph extraction as well as other language understanding tasks.

References

The materials science procedural text corpus. `https://github.com/olivettigroup/annotated-materials-syntheses`. Accessed: 5/4/2019.

Dzmitry Bahdanau, Felix Hill, Jan Leike, Edward Hughes, Pushmeet Kohli, and Edward Grefenstette. 2018. Learning to Understand Goal Specifications by Modelling Reward. pages 1–19.

Trapit Bansal, Arvind Neelakantan, and Andrew McCallum. 2017. RelNet: End-to-end Modeling of Entities & Relations. pages 1–6.

Antoine Bosselut, Omer Levy, Ari Holtzman, Corin Ennis, Dieter Fox, and Yejin Choi. 2018. Simulating action dynamics with neural process networks. *Proceedings of the 6th International Conference for Learning Representations*.

Marc-Alexandre Côté, Ákos Kádár, Xingdi Yuan, Ben Kybartas, Tavian Barnes, Emery Fine, James Moore, Matthew Hausknecht, Layla El Asri, Mahmoud Adada, Wendy Tay, and Adam Trischler. 2018. Textworld: A learning environment for text-based games. *CoRR*, abs/1806.11532.

Rajarshi Das, Tsendsuren Munkhdalai, Xingdi Yuan, Adam Trischler, and Andrew McCallum. 2018. Building Dynamic Knowledge Graphs from Text using Machine Reading Comprehension. pages 1–12.

Wenfeng Feng, Hankz Hankui Zhuo, and Subbarao Kambhampati. 2018. Extracting Action Sequences from Texts Based on Deep Reinforcement Learning.

Jessica B Hamrick. 2019. Analogues of mental simulation and imagination in deep learning. *Current Opinion in Behavioral Sciences*.

Jiarong Jiang, Adam R. Teichert, Hal Daumé, and Jason Eisner. 2012. Learned prioritization for trading off accuracy and speed. In *NIPS*.

Daniel D. Johnson. 2017. Learning graphical state transitions. In *ICLR 2017*.

Daniel Khashabi, Tushar Khot, Ashutosh Sabharwal, and Dan Roth. 2018. Question answering as global reasoning over semantic abstractions. In *AAAI*.

Edward Kim, Zach Jensen, Alexander van Grootel, Kevin Huang, Matthew Staib, Sheshera Mysore, Haw-Shiuan Chang, Emma Strubell, Andrew McCallum, Stefanie Jegelka, and Elsa Olivetti. 2018. Inorganic Materials Synthesis Planning with Literature-Trained Neural Networks.

Omer Levy, Minjoon Seo, Eunsol Choi, and Luke Zettlemoyer. 2017. Zero-Shot Relation Extraction via Reading Comprehension.

Chen Liang, Jonathan Berant, Quoc Le, Kenneth D. Forbus, and Ni Lao. 2016. Neural Symbolic Machines: Learning Semantic Parsers on Freebase with Weak Supervision (Short Version).

Zhengdong Lu, Haotian Cui, Xianggen Liu, Yukun Yan, and Daqi Zheng. 2018. Object-oriented neural programming (oonp) for document understanding. In *ACL*.

Li Lucy and Jon Gauthier. 2017. Are distributional representations ready for the real world? Evaluating word vectors for grounded perceptual meaning.

Adam H. Marblestone, Gregory Wayne, and Konrad P. Körding. 2016. Toward an integration of deep learning and neuroscience. In *Front. Comput. Neurosci.*

Diego Marcheggiani and Laura Perez. 2018. Deep Graph Convolutional Encoders for Structured Data to Text Generation.

Sheshera Mysore, Edward Kim, Emma Strubell, Ao Liu, Haw-Shiuan Chang, Srikrishna Kompella, Kevin Huang, Andrew McCallum, and Elsa Olivetti. 2017. Automatically Extracting Action Graphs from Materials Science Synthesis Procedures.

Karthik Narasimhan. 2017. *Grounding natural language with autonomous interaction*. Ph.D. thesis, Massachusetts Institute of Technology, Cambridge, USA.

Baolin Peng, Xiujun Li, Jianfeng Gao, Jingjing Liu, Kam-Fai Wong, and Shang-Yu Su. 2018. Deep Dyna-Q: Integrating Planning for Task-Completion Dialogue Policy Learning.

Scott Reed and Nando de Freitas. 2015. Neural Programmer-Interpreters. pages 1–13.

Richard S. Sutton. 1990. Integrated Architectures for Learning, Planning, and Reacting Based on Approximating Dynamic Programming. In *Machine Learning Proceedings 1990*.

Terry Winograd. 1972. Understanding natural language. *Cognitive Psychology*, 3(1):1 – 191.

Kexin Yi, Jiajun Wu, Chuang Gan, Antonio Torralba, Pushmeet Kohli, and Joshua B. Tenenbaum. 2018. Neural-Symbolic VQA: Disentangling Reasoning from Vision and Language Understanding. (NeurIPS).

Tom Zahavy, Matan Haroush, Nadav Merlis, Daniel Jaymin Mankowitz, and Shie Mannor. 2018. Learn what not to learn: Action elimination with deep reinforcement learning. In *NeurIPS*.

A Appendices

A.1 Entity & Relation Types

We have claimed that converting an annotation schema to a game for TEXTLABS was relatively straightforward. In this section, we provide details of the mapping between the Synthesis Project annotation schema of (denoted with "SP" in the tables) to the TEXTLABS implementation (denoted "TL"). A mapping between the central entity types is presented in Figure 5, as well as the TEXTLABS actions and representative corresponding relations in the schema. All current TEXTLABS entities and actions are shown here, though not all of the original entities and relations are listed. For the full mapping, refer to the project source repository.

A.2 Synthetic Action-Graphs

Figure 6 displays sample representative generated quests for the various difficulty levels evaluated in Sec. 5, demonstrating the controllable complexity. As can be seen by comparison with the real text in Fig. 7 (which is only one sentence), these graphs correspond to short real-world surfaces, where even the hardest could by covered by a 2-3 sentence-long procedure.

A.3 Action-Graphs from Real Annotated Graphs

We now provide further details on how the original Synthesis Project (SP) annotated graphs can be converted to a TEXTLABS action graph K. There are some minor differences between the formats, primarily in the handling of the SP "next-operation" relation. Rather than use a "next-operation" relation, we currently opt to explicitly model inputs/outputs to operations, as can be seen in Fig. 7. This is a natural abstraction away from the surface text enabled by the grounded environment, and helps in tracking which materials participated in each operation, which is useful information for later analysis. Also, as noted, we currently use a simplified mapping (for example, many descriptor annotations such "Amount-Unit", "Property-Misc", etc. are chunked together as generic descriptors). In Fig. 7 we show K both in action graph and action sequence form to demonstrate the equivalence. Also, we note that the "next-operation" annotations in MSP are currently just placeholders and not the true labels. For the purpose of demonstration, in Fig. 7 we manually add the correct annotation to our example (center and bottom).

Entity Type (SP)	Entity Type (TL)	Notes
Material	Material	
Number	Descriptor	
Operation	Operation	
Amount-Unit	Descriptor	
Condition-Unit	Operation-Descriptor	
Material-Descriptor	Material-Descriptor	
Condition-Misc	Operation-Descriptor	
Synthesis-Apparatus	Synthesis-Apparatus	
Nonrecipe-Material	Null	Currently ignored, not part of synthesis
Brand	Descriptor	
Apparatus-Descriptor	Synthesis-Apparatus-Descriptor	
-	Mixture	Internal entity, represents a mixture
Relation Type (SP)	**Action (TL)**	
Participant-Material	input-assign	
Apparatus-of	locate	
Recipe-Target	obtain	
Descriptor-of	link-descriptor	
-	run-op	Internal, used for simulating actions
-	take/drop/examine	Native TextWorld actions on entities

Figure 5: Central entity/relation types from the Synthesis Project schema ("SP"), and the corresponding TEXT-LABS version ("TL").

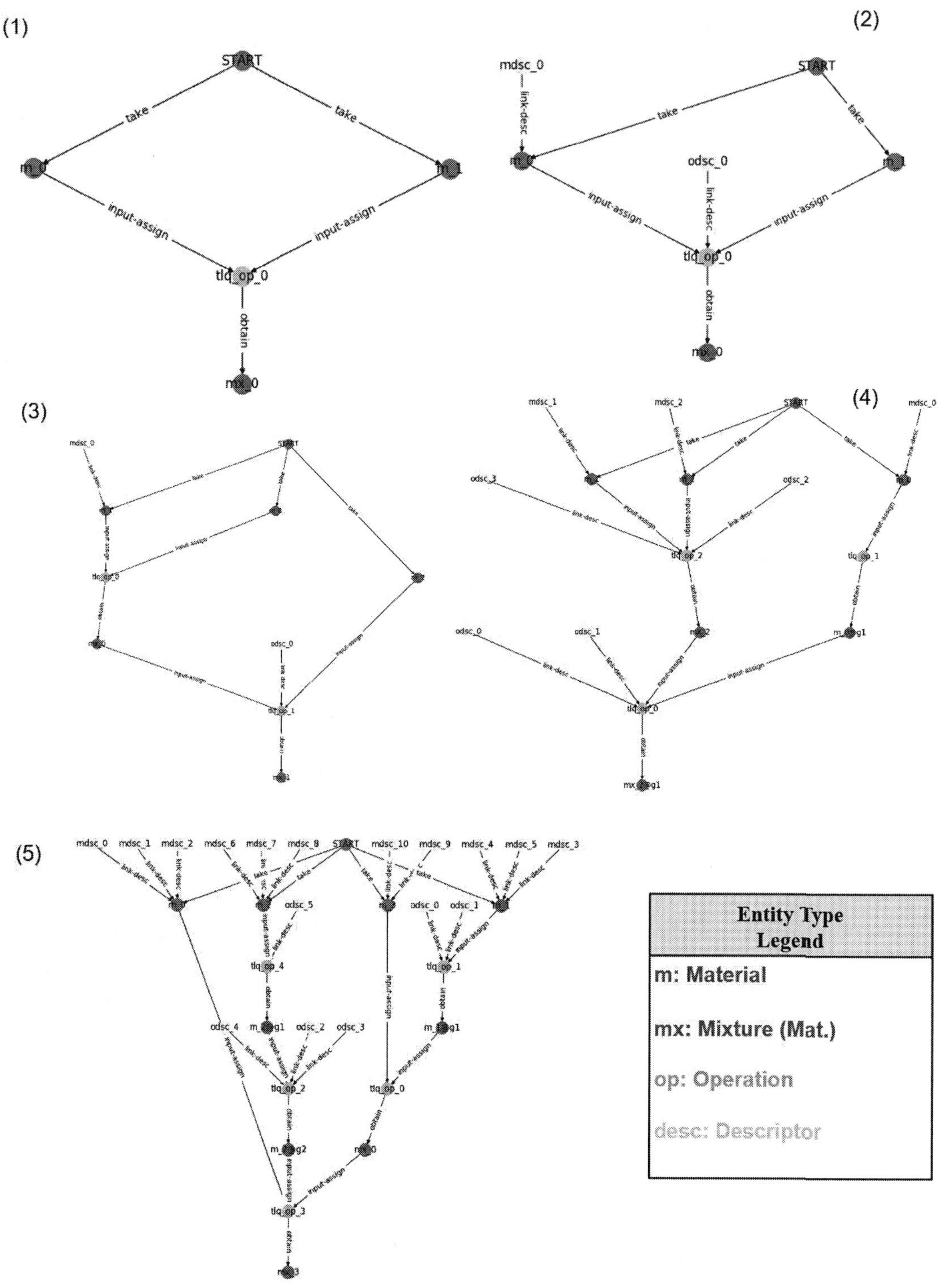

Figure 6: Sample representative generated quests for various difficulty levels (listed in parentheses by each graph). Each edge corresponds to an action in the text-based game.

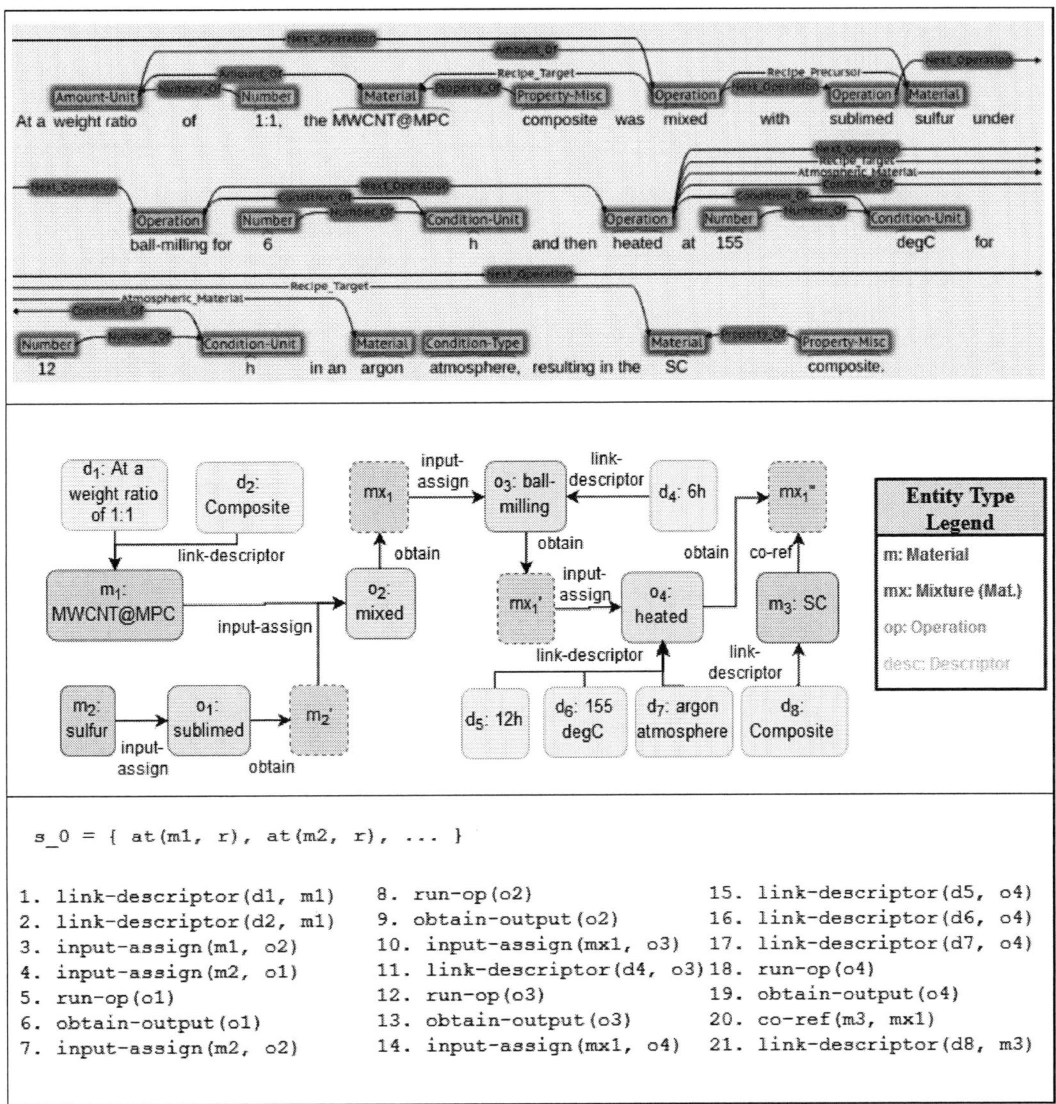

Figure 7: Comparisons of the equivalent action graph representations. **Top**: Action graph section from Synthesis Project (MSP). **Center**: TEXTLABS, showing same section with K in graph form. Dashed borders indicate operation result entities which may be implicit in the text. **Bottom**: TEXTLABS with same K as list of actions from initial state s_0.

Textual and Visual Characteristics of Mathematical Expressions in Scholar Documents

Vidas Daudaravicius

UAB VTeX / Lithuania

`vidas.daudaravicius@vtex.lt`

Abstract

Mathematical expressions (ME) are widely used in scholar documents. In this paper we analyze characteristics of textual and visual MEs characteristics for the image-to-LaTeX translation task. While there are open datasets of LaTeX files with MEs included it is very complicated to extract these MEs from a document and to compile the list of MEs. Therefore we release a corpus of open-access scholar documents with PDF and JATS-XML parallel files. The MEs in these documents are LaTeX encoded and are document independent. The data contains more than 1.2 million distinct annotated formulae and more than 80 million raw tokens of LaTeX MEs in more than 8 thousand documents. While the variety of textual lengths and visual sizes of MEs are not well defined we found that the task of analyzing MEs in scholar documents can be reduced to the subtask of a particular text length, image width and height bounds, and display MEs can be processed as arrays of partial MEs.

1 Introduction

Mathematics is recognized as the most ancient scientific field in the world. Symbols were used from the beginning of mathematics. A specific breakthrough in mathematical language was the invention of the *equals* symbol (=) that is now universally accepted in mathematics, which was first recorded by the Welsh mathematician Robert Recorde in *The Whetstone of Witte* (1557)[1]. Mathematics became the language of symbols to ease mathematical writing, reading and reasoning. Mathematical expressions (ME) are widely used phenomena in scholar documents but we know just little about the textual and visual characteristics of these MEs as this field is less studied in NLP do-

main. The language of MEs is not linear as for instance the English language. Instead, every mathematical symbol has various types of relations, and these relations are vertically and visually represented in 2D space.

The majority of scholar documents is produced in PDF format. The main advantage of this format that it is a universal and human readable format on many devices. PDF also has many advancements for adopting the content of documents for machines by creating *tagged PDF*, though these features are used occasionally. In general, a PDF file contains layout specifications of fonts and their attributes, and no explicit labels are available for mathematics. Many researchers are struggling with the replication of MEs in other documents. Being able to automatically identify and decode mathematics (Lin et al., 2011; Wang and Liu, 2017a,b) in PDF files will enable a wide range of high-level applications such as information retrieval, machine reading, similarity analysis, information aggregation, and reasoning. Siegel et al. (2018) discuss how to recover the positional information of figures in PDF files. The proposed methods could be also used for the alignment of MEs in PDF and XML files. There are also efforts to automatically decode image MEs into LaTeX(Deng et al., 2016, 2017). The length and size of MEs in scholar documents are little discussed. We find that researchers apply specific bounds to the textual length and visual size of MEs without any explanation. Therefore, our interest is to find out specific characteristics of MEs in scholar documents to be used for machine learning.

The *Mathematical REtrieval Collection* (MREC) (Líška et al., 2011) is a subset of the *arXMLiv* corpus and includes documents that were successfully converted to XML. MREC consists of well-formed XHTML documents.

---

[1] `https://en.wikipedia.org/wiki/Equals_sign`

Proceedings of the Workshop on Extracting Structured Knowledge from Scientific Publications, pages 72–81
Minneapolis, USA, June 6, 2019. ©2019 Association for Computational Linguistics

MathML, a W3C standard, is used for representation of mathematical formulas. This corpus contains XHTML files only.

2 Markups and MEs

In general, all MEs in scholar documents can be read out loud as a linear sequence of words. The pseudo-linearity allows to embed MEs into natural language texts despite the visual multidimensional representation. This is a big advantage for humans to be able to combine natural language and symbolic language into one text. But it is not easy for machines to recognize the content and structure of these MEs.

There are several editors and markups for MEs. OpenOffice and MS Office® have internal support for writing MEs using special editors. These editors are frequently used when documents are not highly loaded with MEs, and they are sufficient for most users. The LaTeX typesetting system is used as the main technology in mathematics, physics, and other related domains. LaTeX is widely accepted because of its simplicity for humans to write and read MEs in linear order and to get very complex ME representations. *MathML*[2] is the only standardized markup for MEs which preserves content and layout. Both markups, LaTeX and MathML, are supported by the JATS NISO standard[3]. For instance, the representation of the formula

$$1 - e^{-\frac{1}{2}|x|^2} \tag{1}$$

in LaTeX is:

```
$1-{\mathrm{e}}^{-\frac{1}{2}|x{|}^{2}}$
```

whereas in MathML it is:

```
<mml:math>
<mml:mn>1</mml:mn><mml:mo>-</mml:mo><mml:msup>
<mml:mrow><mml:mi mathvariant="normal">e</mml:mi>
</mml:mrow><mml:mrow><mml:mo>-</mml:mo>
<mml:mstyle displaystyle="false"><mml:mfrac>
<mml:mrow><mml:mn>1</mml:mn></mml:mrow>
<mml:mrow><mml:mn>2</mml:mn></mml:mrow>
</mml:mfrac></mml:mstyle><mml:mo stretchy="false">|
</mml:mo><mml:mi mathvariant="italic">x</mml:mi>
<mml:msup><mml:mrow><mml:mo stretchy="false">|
</mml:mo></mml:mrow><mml:mrow><mml:mn>2</mml:mn>
</mml:mrow></mml:msup></mml:mrow></mml:msup>
</mml:math>.
```

Both representations are equal but the readability for humans and for computers are obviously discrepant. For humans, the LaTeX representation is easy to read, edit and interpret[4]. But LaTeX data

---

[2]Mathematical Markup Language (MathML) Version 3.0 2nd Edition

[3]JATS: Journal Article Tag Suite, version 1.2

[4]The first resource for mathematics zbMATH formula search uses the MathWebSearch system, which is a content-

has no explicit structural representation and advance knowledge is necessary to interpret ME entities and relations. On the other side, MathML data are well structured, relations and bounds of entities are explicitly defined in the data itself. Therefore, we often find both markup representations in scholar documents on-line.

3 Tokenization of LaTeX MEs

In this section we analyze the tokenization task of MEs encoded in LaTeX. Usually, tokenization is the first task of data preprocessing when a long sequence of information is split into words. Frequently, a white-space character is used to separate words. LaTeX allows to use white-space characters in MEs and these white-space characters usually do not affect the visual representation of MEs. For instance,

```
$1-{\mathrm{e}}^{-\frac{1}{2}|x{|}^{2}}$
```

and

```
$ 1 - { \mathrm { e } } ^ { - \frac { 1 }
{ 2 } | x { | } ^ { 2 } } $
```

will result into the same ME image of Formula 1. Sometimes researchers need to insert some text into an ME or use a different approach for encoding variables. Often `\text` or `\mbox` are used for this purpose. The content of these commands is switched into LaTeX mode and, therefore, a white-space character becomes important and influences image rendering. Tokenization by inserting white-spaces

```
$ 1 - { \text { e } } ^ { - \frac { 1 }
{ 2 } | x { | } ^ { \text { 2 } } } $
```

will result to slightly different output:

$$1 - e^{-\frac{1}{2}|x|^2}.$$

White-space characters should not be used straightforwardly for the separation of tokens and should be used with caution. White-space characters should also be included into the vocabulary of ME tokens for the image-to-text task.

Tokenization of MEs is a task of splitting text into minimal meaningful LaTeX tokens, and tokenization should not affect image rendering. A sequence of letters in an ME often denotes a sequence of unique variables visually not split with white-space character. Variables often are single

---

based search engine for MathML formulas based on substituting tree indexing. A query should be inserted in LaTeX, but the database is MathML based.

letters and there is no evident sign for the boundaries of each variable. Single characters and numbers can be used as single tokens in most cases. We suggest to use a TAB or other specific character as a split character for tokenization.

4 The corpus of open-access scholar documents

We collected 8599 open-access scholar documents that are freely accessible on-line, that have both `PDF` and `xhtml` versions, include MEs at least once, and are under CC BY, CC BY NC, or CC BY NC SA licence[5]. The documents were published between 2012 and 2018. The majority of documents are research papers in the following journals:

- *Advances in Difference Equations* (2283 documents)
- *Boundary Value Problems* (1457 documents)
- *Fixed Point Theory and Applications* (1101 documents)
- *Journal of Inequalities and Applications* (2645 documents)

The average number of MEs per document is 291, and the average number of distinct MEs is 193[6]. In Figure 1 we can see that the number of distinct MEs is linearly increasing with the corpus size. This observation shows that the variety of MEs is very complex and new MEs are introduced in each document. This observation is very intriguing as we expected to see the very common distribution called 'heavy tail', Zipf, or other names of the same idea. We also observe that the typical MEs and distinct MEs ratio in each document is similar and equals to 1.5. This means that about 60 percent of MEs are duplicated in the document. The rest of the MEs are unique. The total number of MEs in the corpus is 2.5 million and the number of distinct MEs is 1.2 million. The maximum number of MEs in one document is 2671[7]. There are several documents that have only one ME.

In Figure 2 we observe the vocabulary size in the corpus of MEs. Vocabulary size does not increase significantly when a corpus is doubled from 40 million tokens to 80 million tokens. There are 39 types out of 728 types in total that occur only

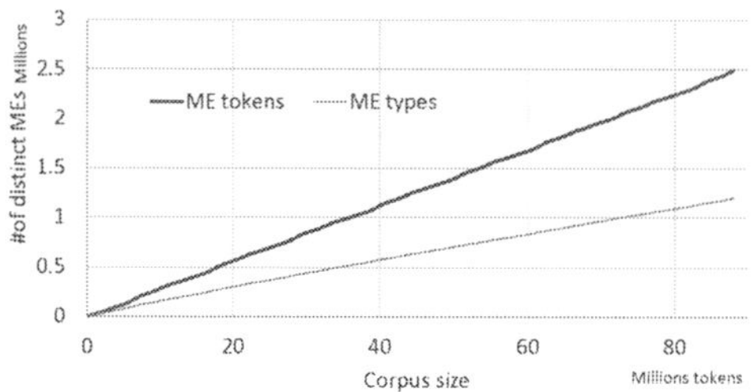

Figure 1: The increase of the number of LaTeX MEs.

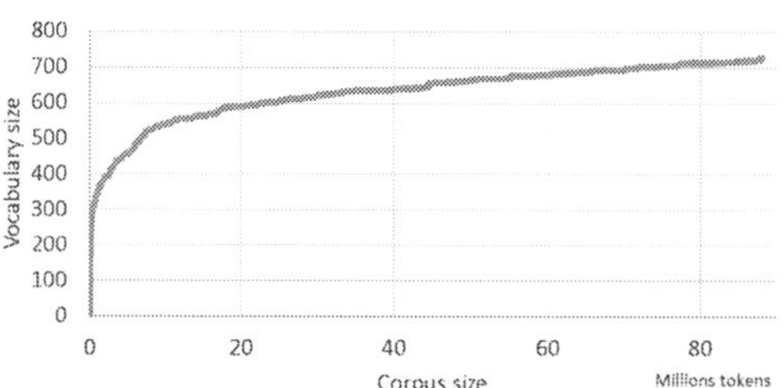

Figure 2: The increase of the vocabulary size of LaTeX tokens.

once in the corpus. And there are 135 types that occur less than ten times in the corpus. The majority in vocabulary are LaTeX commands. The most frequent tokens are {, }, _ and ^. The most frequent LaTeX command is \frac. This shows that the vocabulary of MEs is small and already saturated. We could expect 1000 as vocabulary size upper limit of MEs for very large corpora.

5 Analysis of textual and visual characteristics

In this section we analyze the length of MEs encoded in LaTeX. For the image-to-LaTeX translation task Deng et al. (2017) uses a strict length range which falls in between 40 and 1024 characters and which is limited to 150 tokens. These bounds are used for training data and generated MEs. The paper does not describe the procedure of bounds settings. Do these bounds falsify the real world of MEs and do they consider only some part of the problem?

It is important to differentiate MEs (1) that are used as part of regular text and are placed on the same text line (*inline mode*), and (2) that are placed on a separate line and usually take more than one regular text line (*display mode*). The same ME in *inline* and *display* modes have slightly different visual layout and size. Therefore, we dif-

---

[6]Hereafter, we use JATS XML files to extract LaTeX MEs.

[7]`http://dx.doi.org/10.1186/s13662-015-0541-4`

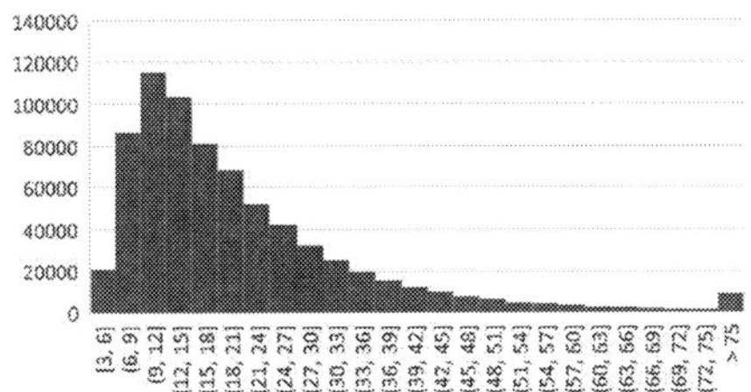

Figure 3: The LaTeX length histogram of inline MEs.

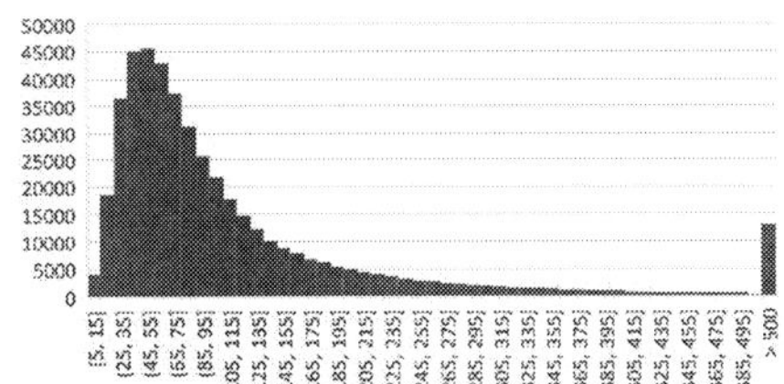

Figure 7: The LaTeX length histogram of display MEs.

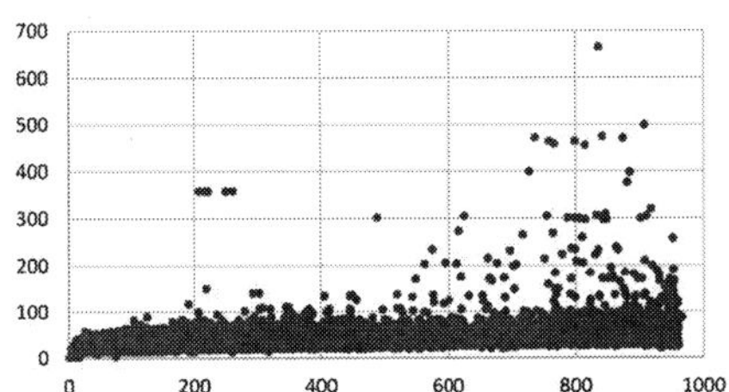

Figure 4: Width (x-axis) and height (y-axis) of rendered inline ME images in pixels (200 dpi).

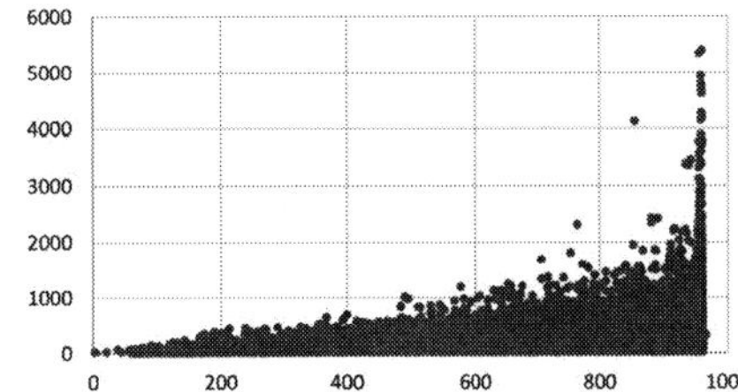

Figure 8: Width (x-axis) and height (y-axis) of rendered display ME images in pixels (200 dpi).

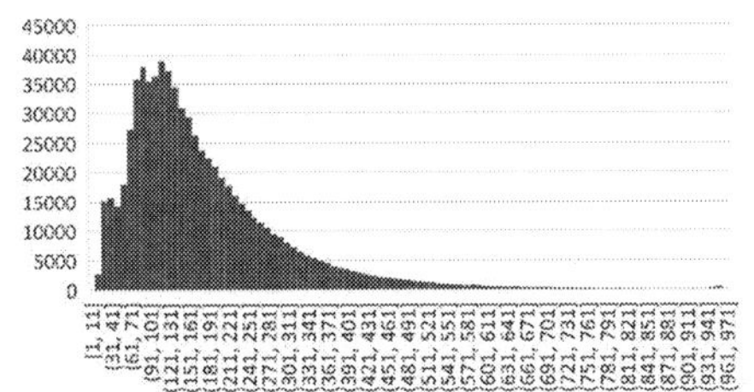

Figure 5: The image width histogram of inline MEs.

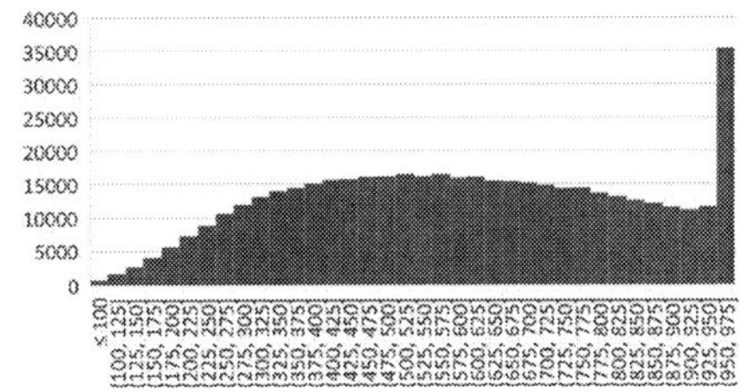

Figure 9: The image width histogram of display MEs.

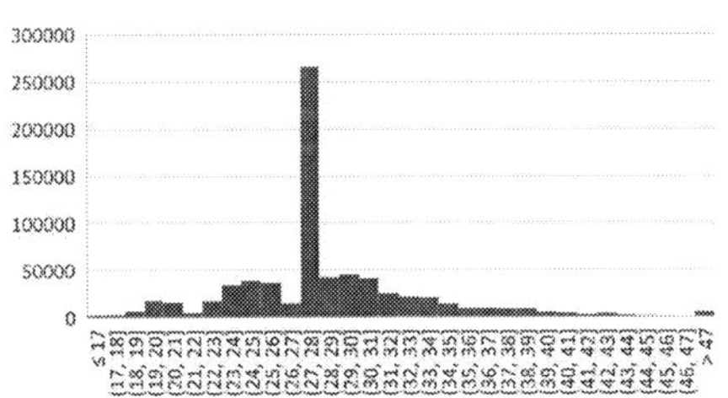

Figure 6: The image height histogram of inline MEs.

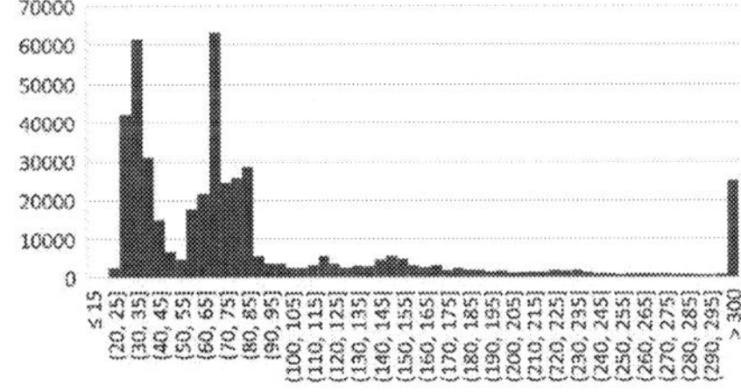

Figure 10: The image height histogram of display MEs.

ferentiate analysis of inline and display MEs.

5.1 Inline MEs

Inline MEs are often short insertions of symbolic language into regular text and they are not spread across many text lines. There are 732498 distinct inline MEs in the corpus. In Figure 3 we observe that the peak length in the list of distinct inline MEs is around 10 tokens and it slowly goes down until 75 tokens. In inline mode formulae that are longer than 75 tokens length we often find an

`\displaystyle` switch which turns inline formulae into display formulae. The longest inline ME is 1008 tokens (see Appendix B). Thus, the upper limit of complex inline formula is around 100 token. The most frequent inline ME is $\{x_n\}$, which occurs 13937 times, and is encoded as `$\{x_{n}\}$` that is 9 tokens length.

We rendered images of all MEs using the `shell` script in Appendix A. Rendered images have 200dpi resolution. In Figure 4 we show a variety of image sizes in pixels. The heights of images fall into the range between 1 and 100 with some odd image height of over 100 pixels. The widths of images are in the range between 1 and 1000 pixels[8]. Figure 4 does not emphasize a specific inline image height and width except the ranges. In Figure 5 we observe the wide range distribution of rendered images. The majority of images are in the range between 30 and 500 pixels. In Figure 6 we observe a specific image height at which the majority of images were rendered. The majority of inline images have a height of 27 or 28 pixels. All other image heights of inline images are less frequent. Therefore, for the ME detection in PDF scholar documents we can expect a formula image size of 30-500 pixels width and 27-28 pixels height. Deng et al. (2017) uses groups of 128, 160, 192, 224, 256, 320, 384, 480 pixels image widths and 32, 64, 96, 128, 160 pixels image heights for the image-to-LaTeX translation task. We can see that image size boxes are very similar to what we observe in our corpus.

5.2 Display MEs

Display MEs are insertions of symbolic language in text and occur in a document as a separate area from the regular text and can be spread over several text lines. There are 467056 distinct display MEs in our corpus. The most frequent display ME occurs 59 times in 55 documents and is 27 tokens length:

$$\lim_{n \to \infty} \|x_{n+1} - x_n\| = 0.$$

This low frequency shows the trend that display MEs are unique and we should not expect occurrence of the same formula in many places. This explains the linear growth of unique MEs in the corpus (see Figure 1). The longest display ME is 13987 tokens length (see Appendix C). Display MEs are very long and many of them can be over 500 tokens in length (see Figure 7). The majority of display formulae range from 20 to 250 tokens. It is definitely much longer than Deng et al. (2017) bound that is 150 tokens.

The display formula image size ranges from 5 to 1000 pixels width and 5 to 6000 pixels height. There is some dependency between the image width and height. If the image height is over 2000 pixels then the image width is always expected to be close to 1000 pixels. In Figure 9 we observe a wide range of frequent image widths and there are many of them at the maximum image width. So,

---

[8] 1000 pixels take the full page width.

the image width mentioned in Deng et al. (2017) is too low for many display MEs. In Figure 10 we observe that the majority of display formulae height is at 30-35 and 65-70 pixels. The image height range between 30-35, which is close to inline formulae image height. This shows that many display formulae fit on a regular text line height. 65-70 pixels height is enough to visualize complex mathematical expressions such as $\sum$ or $\prod$ and it also fit on one line. Display formulae are very complex for the image-to-LaTeX translation task as the text length is much longer than current Deep Neural Networks (DNN) can embed, and image height is too high to feed it to the DNN input. The solution to the problem could be to split display images into arrays of single line display images and to implement the image-to-LaTeX task as a list if partial display images. For this we should also align break points in LaTeX code and images. In general, this is not very complicated as there are clear clues in LaTeX code (e.g., `\\` or `\cr` commands) and in an image (e.g., horizontal gap between lines).

6 Conclusions

We release the corpus of more than 8000 open-access, JATS-NISO-XML tagged and PDF parallel scholar documents which contain at least one mathematical expression. Our analysis shows that inline MEs and display MEs have different textual and visual characteristics. Further, a display mathematical expression should be used as an array of partial mathematical expressions that each fit on one visual line. The textual length of inline MEs ranges between 5 to 75 tokens, image width ranges between 30 to 500 pixels, and image height ranges between 20 to 40 pixels. Display ME textual length ranges from 15 to more than 500 tokens, image width ranges between 100 to 1000 pixels, and image height ranges between 20 to more than 300 pixels. The partial display image height ranges between 20 to 85 pixels. These bounding settings include the majority of all mathematical expressions and can be used for image-to-LaTeX translation task implementation.

Acknowledgments

This work was partially funded by Lithuanian Business Support Agency (Grant No J05-LVPA-K-03-0016).

References

Yuntian Deng, Anssi Kanervisto, Jeffrey Ling, and Alexander M. Rush. 2017. Image-to-markup generation with coarse-to-fine attention. In *Proceedings of the 34th International Conference on Machine Learning*, volume 70 of *Proceedings of Machine Learning Research*, pages 980–989, International Convention Centre, Sydney, Australia. PMLR.

Yuntian Deng, Anssi Kanervisto, and Alexander M. Rush. 2016. What you get is what you see: A visual markup decompiler.

Xiaoyan Lin, Liangcai Gao, Zhi Tang, Xiaofan Lin, and Xuan Hu. 2011. Mathematical formula identification in pdf documents. pages 1419–1423.

Martin Líška, Petr Sojka, Michal Růžička, and Petr Mravec. 2011. Web Interface and Collection for Mathematical Retrieval: WebMIaS and MREC. In *Towards a Digital Mathematics Library.*, pages 77–84, Bertinoro, Italy. Masaryk University.

Noah Siegel, Nicholas Lourie, Russell Power, and Waleed Ammar. 2018. Extracting scientific figures with distantly supervised neural networks. *CoRR*, abs/1804.02445.

Xing Wang and Jyh-Charn Liu. 2017a. A content-constrained spatial (ccs) model for layout analysis of mathematical expressions. pages 334–339.

Xing Wang and Jyh-Charn Liu. 2017b. A font setting based bayesian model to extract mathematical expression in pdf files. pages 759–764.

A   `shell` script for rendering png images with pdflatex

```
#!/bin/sh

cd "$1"
pdflatex -jobname "$2"
  "\documentclass[border=2pt]{standalone}\usepackage{amsmath}\usepackage{amssymb}
   \usepackage{upgreek}\usepackage{mathrsfs}\usepackage{wasysym}
   \usepackage{esint}\usepackage{varwidth} \begin{document}
   \begin{varwidth}{\linewidth}
   $3
   \end{varwidth}\end{document}"

convert -density 200 $2.pdf -quality 100 -colorspace RGB $2.png

convert $2.png -trim $2.png
rm $2.pdf $2.log $2.aux
```

`texlive` and `imagemagic` packages should be on your system to run a sample command:

```
$./formula path filename "$$\sqrt{\frac{1}{2}}$$"
```

B   The longest inline mathematical expression [9]

$A_3 = p_1(a_1 d_1^2 \mu \hat{I}\hat{P} + a_1 d_1 q_1 \mu \hat{I}\hat{P} + a_1 d_1^2 d_2 \hat{I}^2 \hat{P} + a_1 d_1 d_2 q_1 \hat{I}^2 \hat{P} + a_1 d_1^2 q_2 \hat{I}^2 \hat{P} + a_1 d_1 q_1 q_2 \hat{I}^2 \hat{P}) + (p_1 - \tau_1)(a_1 d_1 q_1 \mu \hat{I}\hat{P}) + a_1 q_1^2 \mu \hat{I}\hat{P} + a_1 d_1 d_2 q_1 \hat{I}^2 \hat{P} + a_1 d_2 q_1^2 \hat{I}^2 \hat{P} + a_1 d_1 q_1 q_2 \hat{I}^2 \hat{P} + a_1 q_1^2 q_2 \hat{I}^2 \hat{P}) + p_2(-a_2 d_2^2 r \hat{I}\hat{M} - a_2 d_2 q_2 r \hat{I}\hat{M} - a_2 d_2^2 \gamma \hat{I}\hat{M} - a_2 d_2 q_2 \gamma \hat{I}\hat{M} + a_2 d_1 d_2^2 \hat{I}^2 \hat{M} + a_2 d_2^2 q_1 \hat{I}^2 \hat{M} + a_2 d_1 d_2 q_2 \hat{I}^2 \hat{M} + a_2 d_2 q_1 q_2 \hat{I}^2 \hat{M} + \frac{2 a_2 d_2^2 r \hat{I}\hat{M}\hat{P}}{K} + \frac{2 a_2 d_2 q_2 r \hat{I}\hat{M}\hat{P}}{K} + (p_2 - \tau_2)(a_2 d_2 q_2 r \hat{I}\hat{M} + a_2 q_2^2 r \hat{I}\hat{M} + a_2 d_2 q_2 \gamma \hat{I}\hat{M} + a_2 q_2^2 \gamma \hat{I}\hat{M} - a_2 d_1 d_2 q_2 \hat{I}^2 \hat{M} - a_2 d_2 q_1 q_2 \hat{I}^2 \hat{M} - a_2 d_1 q_2^2 \hat{I}^2 \hat{M} - a_2 q_1 q_2^2 \hat{I}^2 \hat{M} - \frac{2 a_2 d_2 q_2 r \hat{I}\hat{M}\hat{P}}{K} - \frac{2 a_2 q_2^2 r \hat{I}\hat{M}\hat{P}}{K})$

C   The longest display mathematical expression [10]

$$\begin{aligned}
\phi^{(1)} = &-\frac{1}{8} e^{\frac{i}{2}(-x-t\alpha+2t\alpha\beta)} \sqrt{2}\big(-2it^2\alpha^2 - 4t\alpha + 2t^2\alpha^2 + 2x^2 + 1 + i + 4xt\alpha \\
& - 4ixt\alpha - 4ixt\alpha\beta^2 + 4it\alpha\beta^2 - 2t^2\alpha^2\beta^4 - 4x + 2i\alpha^2\beta^4 t^2 \\
& - 4it^2\alpha^2\beta^2 - 4xt\alpha\beta^2 - 4\alpha^2\beta^2 t^2 - 2ix^2\big), \\
\psi^{(1)} = &\frac{i}{8} e^{-\frac{i}{2}(-x-t\alpha+2t\alpha\beta)} \sqrt{2}\big(2x^2 + 4x - 2it^2\alpha^2 + 1 + i \\
& - 4ixt\alpha + 4t\alpha + 2t^2\alpha^2 - 4it\alpha\beta^2 - 4xt\alpha\beta^2 - 4\alpha^2\beta^2 t^2 \\
& - 4ixt\alpha\beta^2 + 2i\alpha^2\beta^4 t^2 + 4xt\alpha - 4it^2\alpha^2\beta^2 - 2ix^2 - 2t^2\alpha^2\beta^4\big), \\
\phi^{(2)} = &-\frac{1}{192} e^{\frac{i}{2}(-x-t\alpha+2t\alpha\beta)} \sqrt{2}\big(-12 + 48t^2\alpha^2\beta^2 + 60x - 24xt\alpha + 8it^3\alpha^3\beta^6 + 8t^3\alpha^3 \\
& + 36it\alpha\beta^2 - 24t^3\alpha^3\beta^2 + 8t^3\alpha^3\beta^6 + 24x^2t\alpha + 24xt^2\alpha^2 - 24t^3\alpha^3\beta^4 + 48b_1 \\
& - 48ixt^3\alpha^3\beta^4 + 240ixt\alpha - 24xt^2\alpha^2\beta^4 - 24x^2t\alpha\beta^2 - 48xt^2\alpha^2\beta^2 + 12\alpha\beta^2 t \\
& + 60t\alpha - 12x^2 - 12t^2\alpha^2 + 48xt\alpha\beta^2 + 48t\alpha\beta^2 b_1 - 48t\alpha\beta^2 d_1 + 48x^2t^2\alpha^2\beta^2 \\
& + 48xt^3\alpha^3\beta^2 - 16t^3\alpha^3\beta^6 x + 16x^3t\alpha\beta^2 - 48b_1 x - 48xd_1 - 48t\alpha b_1 - 48t\alpha d_1 \\
& + 12t^2\alpha^2\beta^4 + 16t^4\alpha^4\beta^2 - 16t^4\alpha^4\beta^6 + 120ix^2 - 24ix^2t^2\alpha^2\beta^4 + 48it\alpha\beta^2 d_1 \\
& - 48ixt^2\alpha^2\beta^2 - 24ix^2t\alpha\beta^2 - 24it^4\alpha^4\beta^4 + 24it^2\alpha^2\beta^2 - 24ixt^2\alpha^2 + 8x^3 \\
& - 24ix^2t\alpha + 48id_1 + 48it\alpha\beta^2 b_1 + 4ix^4 + 24ix^2t^2\alpha^2 + 48it\alpha b_1 + 24ixt\alpha\beta^2 \\
& + 24ixt^2\alpha^2\beta^4 + 24it^3\alpha^3\beta^4 - 8ix^3 + 15i - 84ix + 72it^2\alpha^2\beta^4 - 48it\alpha d_1 \\
& - 24it^3\alpha^3\beta^2 + 16ix^3t\alpha + 4it^4\alpha^4\beta^8 + 120it^2\alpha^2 + 48ib_1 x + 4it^4\alpha^4
\end{aligned}$$

---

[9] See the original formula at Chaudhary, M., Pathak, R. *A dynamical approach to the legal and illegal logging of forestry population and conservation using taxation* Advances in Difference Equations (2017) 2017:385.

[10] See the original formula at Wen *Advances in Difference Equations* (2016) 2016:311. This kind of formula is automatically generated by the specific algorithms to mathematically describe some phenomenon.

$$- 84it\alpha - 8it^3\alpha^3 - 48ixd_1 + 16it^3\alpha^3 x\big),$$

$$\psi^{(2)} = \frac{i}{192} e^{-\frac{i}{2}(-x-t\alpha+2t\alpha\beta)} \sqrt{2}\big(-12 + 48t^2\alpha^2\beta^2 - 60x - 24xt\alpha - 8t^3\alpha^3 + 24t^3\alpha^3\beta^2$$
$$- 8t^3\alpha^3\beta^6 - 24x^2 t\alpha - 24xt^2\alpha^2 + 24t^3\alpha^3\beta^4 - 48b_1 - 36it\alpha\beta^2 + 16it^3\alpha^3 x$$
$$+ 24xt^2\alpha^2\beta^4 + 24x^2 t\alpha\beta^2 + 48xt^2\alpha^2\beta^2 - 12\alpha\beta^2 t - 60t\alpha - 12x^2 - 12t^2\alpha^2$$
$$+ 48xt\alpha\beta^2 + 48t\alpha\beta^2 b_1 - 48t\alpha\beta^2 d_1 + 48x^2 t^2\alpha^2\beta^2 + 48xt^3\alpha^3\beta^2 - 16t^3\alpha^3\beta^6 x$$
$$+ 16x^3 t\alpha\beta^2 - 48b_1 x - 48xd_1 - 48t\alpha b_1 - 48t\alpha d_1 + 12t^2\alpha^2\beta^4 + 16t^4\alpha^4\beta^2$$
$$- 16t^4\alpha^4\beta^6 - 24ixt^2\alpha^2\beta^4 + 24ix^2 t\alpha + 48it\alpha\beta^2 b_1 - 48it\alpha d_1 + 48it\alpha b_1$$
$$+ 24it^3\alpha^3\beta^2 - 24ix^2 t^2\alpha^2\beta^4 + 120it^2\alpha^2 + 48ib_1 x - 24it^3\alpha^3\beta^4 + 240ixt\alpha$$
$$+ 48ixt^2\alpha^2\beta^2 + 72it^2\alpha^2\beta^4 + 120ix^2 - 48ixt^3\alpha^3\beta^4 + 24it^2\alpha^2\beta^2 + 16ix^3 t\alpha$$
$$+ 8ix^3 - 8x^3 - 8it^3\alpha^3\beta^6 + 48it\alpha\beta^2 d_1 + 84ix - 48id_1 + 24ixt^2\alpha^2$$
$$+ 15i + 24ix^2 t\alpha\beta^2 + 4it^4\alpha^4\beta^8 + 84it\alpha - 24it^4\alpha^4\beta^4 + 24ix^2 t^2\alpha^2 + 4ix^4$$
$$+ 4it^4\alpha^4 - 48ixd_1 + 8it^3\alpha^3 + 24ixt\alpha\beta^2\big),$$

$$\phi^{(3)} = -\frac{1}{23{,}040} e^{\frac{i}{2}(-x-t\alpha+2t\alpha\beta)} \sqrt{2}\big(-405 - 1{,}440x^2 d_1 - 1{,}440b_1 x^2 - 5{,}760ixd_2$$
$$+ 8t^6\alpha^6\beta^1 2 - 48t^6\alpha^6\beta^2 + 48it^5\alpha^5 - 8{,}100t^2\alpha^2\beta^2 - 6{,}840x^2 t^2\alpha^2 + 2{,}880x$$
$$- 120t^6\alpha^6\beta^8 - 1{,}440ib_1^2 + 1{,}440id_1^2 + 3{,}840ix^3 - 8ix^6 - 17{,}010ix^2 - 1{,}260ix^4$$
$$+ 5{,}760id_2 + 48ix^5 - 1{,}440it\alpha\beta^2 b_1 - 5{,}760t\alpha b_2 - 4{,}560xt^3\alpha^3 + 5{,}760ib_2 x$$
$$- 120t^4\alpha^4 x^2 + 1{,}080t^4\alpha^4\beta^4 + 48it^5\alpha^5\beta^1 0x - 2{,}880ixt^2\alpha^2 b_1 - 25{,}380xt\alpha$$
$$- 17{,}010it^2\alpha^2 - 1{,}440ix^2 d_1 + 240t^3\alpha^3 - 2{,}880ixd_1 t\alpha + 1{,}440it^2\alpha^2\beta^4 d_1$$
$$+ 2{,}880it^3\alpha^3\beta^4 b_1 - 2{,}880it^3\alpha^3 d_1\beta^2 + 2{,}880it^2\alpha^2\beta^4 b_1 x - 2{,}880ix^2 t\alpha b_1$$
$$- 2{,}880ix^2 t\alpha\beta^2 d_1 - 5{,}760ixd_1 t^2\alpha^2\beta^2 - 720ix^2 t\alpha\beta^2 - 1{,}440ixt^2\alpha^2\beta^2$$
$$+ 2{,}880id_1 b_1 - 480it^4\alpha^4\beta^6 x^2 + 480ix^2 t^4\alpha^4\beta^2 + 240it^5\alpha^5\beta^2 x + 240ix^4 t^2\alpha^2\beta^2$$
$$+ 1{,}200it^3\alpha^3\beta^6 x - 120it^4\alpha^4\beta^8 x^2 + 480ixt^5\alpha^5\beta^4 + 720ix^2 t^4\alpha^4\beta^4$$
$$+ 480ix^3 t^3\alpha^3\beta^4 + 48ix^5 t\alpha\beta^2 + 5{,}220ixt\alpha\beta^2 + 7{,}920ixt^3\alpha^3\beta^2 + 7{,}920ix^2 t^2\alpha^2\beta^2$$
$$+ 2{,}640ix^3 t\alpha\beta^2 + 120ix^4 t^2\alpha^2\beta^4 - 240it^5\alpha^5\beta^8 x - 480ix^3 t^2\alpha^2\beta^4$$
$$+ 240it^4\alpha^4\beta^8 x - 14{,}400ib_1 x - 1{,}440ixt^4\alpha^4\beta^4 - 1{,}440ix^2 t^3\alpha^3\beta^4 - 4{,}560x^3 t\alpha$$
$$+ 2{,}880ib_1 xt\alpha\beta^2 + 2{,}880it^2\alpha^2 b_1\beta^2 + 5{,}760t^3\alpha^3\beta^2 + 1{,}920t^3\alpha^3\beta^6 + 720x^2 t\alpha$$
$$+ 720xt^2\alpha^2 - 720t^3\alpha^3\beta^4 + 13{,}140ix - 3{,}600b_1 - 5{,}040d_1 + 5{,}760b_2$$
$$- 5{,}760t\alpha d_2 - 960ix^3 b_1 - 160it^3\alpha^3\beta^6 x^3 - 8it^6\alpha^6 + 1{,}800ix^2 t^2\alpha^2\beta^4$$
$$+ 1{,}440ib_1 x^2 + 3{,}840it^3\alpha^3 - 720xt^2\alpha^2\beta^4 + 5{,}760x^2 t\alpha\beta^2 + 11{,}520xt^2\alpha^2\beta^2$$
$$+ 1{,}620\alpha\beta^2 t + 1{,}440ixd_1 + 2{,}880t\alpha - 1{,}260it^4\alpha^4 - 12{,}690x^2 - 12{,}690t^2\alpha^2$$
$$- 120x^4 t^2\alpha^2 + 11{,}520ix^2 t\alpha - 8{,}100xt\alpha\beta^2 - 2{,}880t\alpha\beta^2 b_1 + 1{,}440t\alpha\beta^2 d_1$$
$$- 9{,}360x^2 t^2\alpha^2\beta^2 - 9{,}360xt^3\alpha^3\beta^2 + 2{,}160t^3\alpha^3\beta^4 x - 720t^3\alpha^3\beta^6 x - 3{,}120x^3 t\alpha\beta^2$$
$$+ 1{,}080x^2 t^2\alpha^2\beta^4 - 1{,}140t^4\alpha^4 + 1{,}440b_1 x + 14{,}400xd_1 - 1{,}140x^4 + 780t^4\alpha^4\beta^8$$
$$+ 1{,}440t\alpha b_1 + 14{,}400t\alpha d_1 + 4{,}050t^2\alpha^2\beta^4 - 3{,}120t^4\alpha^4\beta^2 - 720t^4\alpha^4\beta^6$$
$$+ 240it^3\alpha^3\beta^6 - 720it^3\alpha^3\beta^2 + 240ix^4 t\alpha + 13{,}140it\alpha + 11{,}520ixt^2\alpha^2$$
$$- 2{,}880xt\alpha\beta^2 d_1 - 1{,}440it^2\alpha^2 d_1 + 480ix^3 t^2\alpha^2 + 480it^3\alpha^3 x^2 + 240it^5\alpha^5\beta^8$$
$$- 5{,}040it^3\alpha^3 x - 34{,}020ixt\alpha - 5{,}040ix^3 t\alpha + 2{,}610it^2\alpha^2\beta^4 + 1{,}440it\alpha d_1$$
$$+ 660it^4\alpha^4\beta^8 - 7{,}560ix^2 t^2\alpha^2 - 1{,}440t^2\alpha^2 b_1 + 240t^5\alpha^5\beta^2 - 480t^5\alpha^5\beta^6$$

$$+\,48t^5\alpha^5\beta^10 - 1{,}440t^2\alpha^2 d_1 + 960x^3 d_1 - 5{,}760b_2 x - 5{,}760xd_2 + 2{,}880d_1 b_1$$

$$+\,1{,}440b_1^2 - 8x^6 - 1{,}440d_1^2 + 5{,}760t\alpha\beta^2 b_2 - 5{,}760t\alpha\beta^2 d_2 + 2{,}880x^2 t\alpha d_1$$

$$+\,2{,}880xt^2\alpha^2 d_1 - 2{,}880t^3\alpha^3\beta^4 d_1 - 2{,}880t^3\alpha^3\beta^2 b_1 + 960t^3\alpha^3\beta^6 b_1 - 48x^5 t\alpha\beta^2$$

$$+\,160t^6\alpha^6\beta^6 - 160t^3\alpha^3 x^3 - 48t^5\alpha^5 x - 48t^6\alpha^6\beta^10 + 960t^3\alpha^3 d_1 - 48x^5 t\alpha$$

$$+\,120t^6\alpha^6\beta^4 - 2{,}880x^2 t\alpha\beta^2 b_1 - 5{,}760xt^2\alpha^2\beta^2 b_1 - 2{,}880xt^2\alpha^2\beta^4 d_1 - 8t^6\alpha^6$$

$$-\,240t^5\alpha^5\beta^2 x + 480t^5\alpha^5\beta^6 x - 240x^4 t^2\alpha^2\beta^2 - 480x^3 t^3\alpha^3\beta^2 + 480x^3 t^3\alpha^3\beta^4$$

$$-\,480x^2 t^4\alpha^4\beta^2 + 720x^2 t^4\alpha^4\beta^4 + 480xt^5\alpha^5\beta^4 + 160t^3\alpha^3\beta^6 x^3 + 480t^4\alpha^4\beta^6 x^2$$

$$-\,120t^4\alpha^4\beta^8 x^2 - 240t^5\alpha^5\beta^8 x + 120x^4 t^2\alpha^2\beta^4 - 48t^5\alpha^5\beta^10 x - 14{,}400it\alpha b_1$$

$$-\,960it^3\alpha^3 b_1 + 3{,}600ixt^3\alpha^3\beta^4 + 480ix^3 t^3\alpha^3\beta^2 + 5{,}220it^2\alpha^2\beta^2 - 48ix^5 t\alpha$$

$$+\,5{,}760it\alpha b_2 - 160it^3\alpha^3 x^3 - 120it^4\alpha^4 x^2 - 120ix^4 t^2\alpha^2 - 48it^5\alpha^5 x - 120it^6\alpha^6\beta^8$$

$$+\,120it^6\alpha^6\beta^4 + 240x^4 t\alpha\beta^2 - 2{,}880xt\alpha b_1 - 2{,}880t^2\alpha^2\beta^2 d_1 + 8it^6\alpha^6\beta^12$$

$$+\,1{,}200it^4\alpha^4\beta^6 + 2{,}640it^4\alpha^4\beta^2 - 160it^6\alpha^6\beta^6 + 48it^6\alpha^6\beta^2 - 480it^5\alpha^5\beta^4$$

$$+\,240it^4\alpha^4 x + 1{,}800it^4\alpha^4\beta^4 - 5{,}760it\alpha d_2 + 48it^6\alpha^6\beta^10 + 1{,}440it^2\alpha^2 b_1$$

$$+\,240x^3 + 2{,}880it^2\alpha^2\beta^2 d_1 + 2{,}880ixt\alpha\beta^2 d_1 - 1{,}440it^2\alpha^2\beta^4 b_1 + 1{,}440t^2\alpha^2\beta^4 b_1$$

$$-\,2{,}880xt\alpha d_1 + 2{,}880t^2\alpha^2\beta^2 b_1 + 1{,}440t^2\alpha^2\beta^4 d_1 + 960x^3 t^2\alpha^2\beta^2$$

$$+\,1{,}440x^2 t^3\alpha^3\beta^2 + 960xt^4\alpha^4\beta^2 - 480t^3\alpha^3\beta^6 x^2 - 960t^4\alpha^4\beta^6 x - 3{,}600id_1$$

$$-\,2{,}880it\alpha\beta^2 d_1 + 5{,}760it\alpha\beta^2 b_2 + 2{,}880ib_1 xt\alpha - 1{,}395i + 5{,}040ib_1$$

$$+\,2{,}880xt\alpha\beta^2 b_1 + 960it^3\alpha^3\beta^6 d_1 - 480it^5\alpha^5\beta^6 x + 5{,}760it\alpha\beta^2 d_2 \big),$$

$$\psi^{(3)} = \frac{i}{23{,}040}\, e^{-\frac{i}{2}(-x - t\alpha + 2t\alpha\beta)}\sqrt{2}\big(-405 + 720it^3\alpha^3\beta^2 + 1{,}440x^2 d_1 + 1{,}440b_1 x^2$$

$$+\,8t^6\alpha^6\beta^12 - 48t^6\alpha^6\beta^2 - 8{,}100t^2\alpha^2\beta^2 - 6{,}840x^2 t^2\alpha^2 - 2{,}880x$$

$$+\,480ix^3 t^2\alpha^2\beta^4 - 120t^6\alpha^6\beta^8 - 1{,}440ib_1^2 - 5{,}760ixd_1 t^2\alpha^2\beta^2 - 5{,}760ixd_2$$

$$-\,5{,}760t\alpha b_2 - 4{,}560xt^3\alpha^3 + 2{,}880id_1 b_1 - 2{,}880ixt^2\alpha^2 b_1 - 120t^4\alpha^4 x^2$$

$$+\,1{,}080t^4\alpha^4\beta^4 - 25{,}380xt\alpha + 7{,}920ixt^3\alpha^3\beta^2 + 48it^5\alpha^5\beta^10 x - 17{,}010it^2\alpha^2$$

$$-\,240t^3\alpha^3 - 2{,}880ixt\alpha\beta^2 d_1 - 1{,}260ix^4 - 4{,}560x^3 t\alpha - 5{,}760t^3\alpha^3\beta^2$$

$$-\,1{,}920t^3\alpha^3\beta^6 - 720x^2 t\alpha - 720xt^2\alpha^2 + 720t^3\alpha^3\beta^4 + 5{,}760it\alpha b_2 + 3{,}600b_1$$

$$+\,5{,}040d_1 - 5{,}760b_2 - 5{,}760t\alpha d_2 + 5{,}760ib_2 x + 1{,}800ix^2 t^2\alpha^2\beta^4 - 5{,}040ix^3 t\alpha$$

$$-\,240it^5\alpha^5\beta^8 - 160it^3\alpha^3\beta^6 x^3 - 2{,}880it\alpha\beta^2 d_1 - 5{,}040it^3\alpha^3 x - 1{,}440it\alpha\beta^2 b_1$$

$$+\,720xt^2\alpha^2\beta^4 - 5{,}760x^2 t\alpha\beta^2 - 11{,}520xt^2\alpha^2\beta^2 - 1{,}620\alpha\beta^2 t - 2{,}880t\alpha - 8it^6\alpha^6$$

$$-\,12{,}690x^2 - 12{,}690t^2\alpha^2 - 120x^4 t^2\alpha^2 + 120ix^4 t^2\alpha^2\beta^4 + 240it^5\alpha^5\beta^2 x$$

$$-\,8{,}100xt\alpha\beta^2 - 2{,}880t\alpha\beta^2 b_1 + 1{,}440t\alpha\beta^2 d_1 - 9{,}360x^2 t^2\alpha^2\beta^2 - 9{,}360xt^3\alpha^3\beta^2$$

$$+\,2{,}160t^3\alpha^3\beta^4 x - 720t^3\alpha^3\beta^6 x - 3{,}120x^3 t\alpha\beta^2 + 1{,}080x^2 t^2\alpha^2\beta^4 - 1{,}140t^4\alpha^4$$

$$+\,1{,}440b_1 x + 14{,}400xd_1 - 1{,}140x^4 + 780t^4\alpha^4\beta^8 + 1{,}440t\alpha b_1 + 14{,}400t\alpha d_1$$

$$+\,4{,}050t^2\alpha^2\beta^4 - 3{,}120t^4\alpha^4\beta^2 - 720t^4\alpha^4\beta^6 + 2{,}880xt\alpha\beta^2 d_1 - 480it^5\alpha^5\beta^6 x$$

$$-\,160it^3\alpha^3 x^3 + 1{,}440ixt^2\alpha^2\beta^2 - 1{,}440ib_1 x^2 - 48it^5\alpha^5 + 1{,}440t^2\alpha^2 b_1$$

$$-\,240t^5\alpha^5\beta^2 + 480t^5\alpha^5\beta^6 - 48t^5\alpha^5\beta^10 + 1{,}440t^2\alpha^2 d_1 + 960x^3 d_1 - 5{,}760b_2 x$$

$$-\,5{,}760xd_2 + 2{,}880d_1 b_1 + 1{,}440b_1^2 - 8x^6 - 1{,}440d_1^2 + 5{,}760t\alpha\beta^2 b_2$$

$$-\,5{,}760t\alpha\beta^2 d_2 + 2{,}880x^2 t\alpha d_1 + 2{,}880xt^2\alpha^2 d_1 - 2{,}880t^3\alpha^3\beta^4 d_1$$

$$-\,2{,}880t^3\alpha^3\beta^2 b_1 + 960t^3\alpha^3\beta^6 b_1 - 48x^5 t\alpha\beta^2 + 160t^6\alpha^6\beta^6 - 160t^3\alpha^3 x^3$$

$$-\,48t^5\alpha^5 x - 48t^6\alpha^6\beta^10 + 960t^3\alpha^3 d_1 - 48x^5 t\alpha + 120t^6\alpha^6\beta^4 - 2{,}880x^2 t\alpha\beta^2 b_1$$

$$- 5{,}760xt^2\alpha^2\beta^2 b_1 - 2{,}880xt^2\alpha^2\beta^4 d_1 - 8t^6\alpha^6 - 240t^5\alpha^5\beta^2 x + 480t^5\alpha^5\beta^6 x$$

$$- 1{,}260it^4\alpha^4 - 240x^4t^2\alpha^2\beta^2 - 480x^3t^3\alpha^3\beta^2 + 480x^3t^3\alpha^3\beta^4 - 480x^2t^4\alpha^4\beta^2$$

$$+ 720x^2t^4\alpha^4\beta^4 + 480xt^5\alpha^5\beta^4 + 160t^3\alpha^3\beta^6 x^3 + 480t^4\alpha^4\beta^6 x^2 - 120t^4\alpha^4\beta^8 x^2$$

$$- 240t^5\alpha^5\beta^8 x + 120x^4t^2\alpha^2\beta^4 - 48t^5\alpha^5\beta^{10}x + 48ix^5 t\alpha\beta^2 + 2{,}640ix^3 t\alpha\beta^2$$

$$+ 48it^6\alpha^6\beta^{10} + 480it^5\alpha^5\beta^4 - 2{,}880it^3\alpha^3 d_1\beta^2 + 1{,}440ixt^4\alpha^4\beta^4 - 48ix^5$$

$$- 120it^6\alpha^6\beta^8 - 240x^4 t\alpha\beta^2 + 2{,}880xt\alpha b_1 + 2{,}880t^2\alpha^2\beta^2 d_1 - 120it^4\alpha^4\beta^8 x^2$$

$$- 480it^4\alpha^4\beta^6 x^2 + 7{,}920ix^2t^2\alpha^2\beta^2 - 960it^3\alpha^3 b_1 + 2{,}880it^2\alpha^2\beta^4 b_1 x - 8ix^6$$

$$- 7{,}560ix^2t^2\alpha^2 + 2{,}640it^4\alpha^4\beta^2 - 240x^3 - 48ix^5 t\alpha + 960it^3\alpha^3\beta^6 d_1$$

$$+ 48it^6\alpha^6\beta^2 + 1{,}440it\alpha d_1 - 14{,}400ib_1 x - 14{,}400it\alpha b_1 + 5{,}760it\alpha\beta^2 d_2$$

$$+ 5{,}220ixt\alpha\beta^2 - 2{,}880ib_1 xt\alpha\beta^2 + 1{,}440ix^2t^3\alpha^3\beta^4 - 1{,}440t^2\alpha^2\beta^4 b_1$$

$$+ 2{,}880xt\alpha d_1 - 2{,}880t^2\alpha^2\beta^2 b_1 - 1{,}440t^2\alpha^2\beta^4 d_1 - 960x^3t^2\alpha^2\beta^2$$

$$- 1{,}440x^2t^3\alpha^3\beta^2 - 960xt^4\alpha^4\beta^2 + 480t^3\alpha^3\beta^6 x^2 + 960t^4\alpha^4\beta^6 x + 480ixt^5\alpha^5\beta^4$$

$$- 120it^4\alpha^4 x^2 - 13{,}140it\alpha + 3{,}600ixt^3\alpha^3\beta^4 - 2{,}880ix^2 t\alpha b_1 + 8it^6\alpha^6\beta^{12}$$

$$- 5{,}040ib_1 - 2{,}880ix^2 t\alpha\beta^2 d_1 - 160it^6\alpha^6\beta^6 - 5{,}760it\alpha d_2 - 240it^3\alpha^3\beta^6$$

$$- 13{,}140ix + 1{,}200it^3\alpha^3\beta^6 x - 480ix^3t^2\alpha^2 + 1{,}440ixd_1 + 1{,}200it^4\alpha^4\beta^6$$

$$- 34{,}020ixt\alpha - 2{,}880it^2\alpha^2\beta^2 d_1 - 1{,}440it^2\alpha^2\beta^4 d_1 + 5{,}760it\alpha\beta^2 b_2$$

$$- 2{,}880xt\alpha\beta^2 b_1 + 480ix^3t^3\alpha^3\beta^4 + 720ix^2 t\alpha\beta^2 - 48it^5\alpha^5 x - 11{,}520ixt^2\alpha^2$$

$$+ 240ix^4t^2\alpha^2\beta^2 - 2{,}880ib_1 xt\alpha - 3{,}840it^3\alpha^3 - 3{,}840ix^3 + 1{,}440it^2\alpha^2 d_1$$

$$- 5{,}760id_2 + 120it^6\alpha^6\beta^4 + 2{,}880ixd_1 t\alpha + 480ix^3t^3\alpha^3\beta^2 - 2{,}880it^2\alpha^2 b_1\beta^2$$

$$- 120ix^4t^2\alpha^2 + 660it^4\alpha^4\beta^8 - 480it^3\alpha^3 x^2 + 1{,}440ix^2 d_1 + 2{,}880it^3\alpha^3\beta^4 b_1$$

$$+ 1{,}440it^2\alpha^2\beta^4 b_1 + 480ix^2t^4\alpha^4\beta^2 - 1{,}440it^2\alpha^2 b_1 - 240it^5\alpha^5\beta^8 x - 240it^4\alpha^4 x$$

$$+ 720ix^2t^4\alpha^4\beta^4 + 1{,}800it^4\alpha^4\beta^4 - 17{,}010ix^2 - 1{,}395i + 1{,}440id_1^2 + 3{,}600id_1$$

$$- 11{,}520ix^2 t\alpha - 960ix^3 b_1 + 2{,}610it^2\alpha^2\beta^4 - 240it^4\alpha^4\beta^8 x$$

$$- 240ix^4 t\alpha + 5{,}220it^2\alpha^2\beta^2\big).$$

Author Index

Association for Computational Linguistics
209 N. Eighth Street
Stroudsburg, Pennsylvania 18360

ISBN 978-1-5108-8780-0